The
Catacombs
of
Paris

The Catacombs of Paris

GILLES THOMAS

Translated and adapted
from the French by
DIANE LANGLUMÉ

Photographs
EMMANUEL GAFFARD

PARIGRAMME

One of the arrows marking the former Ossuary path, no longer used by visitors, as today's itinerary is one-way only.

1

An Underground World Opens Up ❘ 11

2

The Visitor's Itinerary ❘ 43

The Catacombs Ossuary with the Croix de Bordeaux in the background.

"View of Place Saint-Laurent", Cloquet's engraving n° 2. The *pilier à bras* décor fashioned from long bones has now vanished.

1
AN
UNDERGROUND
WORLD
OPENS UP

The Catacombs were long unknown to the public at large. Little did Parisian locals and visitors once imagine that they were treading over the void spaces of the city's former quarries.

It was not until a brochure by Louis Étienne François Héricart Ferrand, Viscount of Thury (the second General Quarry Inspector) first advertised their

⬆ Portrait of the developer of the Catacombs responsible for their being opened up to the public: Héricart de Thury (1776–1854).

existence in 1810 that they began drawing Parisians and tourists. In the 1830s–1840s, visits were not limited to the Ossuary as such. Over this period, *"the itinerary was not fixed; visitors were shown around by men in charge of the Quarry Inspection workshops who* *guided them as struck their fancy; inevitable abuses occurred, the quarry galleries as well as the ossuary were damaged by unscrupulous people and visitors lost their way."*[1] This led to the galleries being shut down for a few years. Paris, the City of Lights, has its share of darkness. Underground, another world has developed, an almost parallel universe, which nevertheless remains intimately linked to the world aboveground:

1   Émile Gérards, *Paris souterrain*, Torcy, DMI, 1991, p.462.

← At the Catacombs entrance, visitors could once buy candles and holders. (*Journal illustré*, 1875).

↓ In 1903, twenty-five English visitors lost their way by straying from the tourist path, for the Catacombs were not cut off from the rest of the quarries (*Le Pèlerin*, November 1903).

a shadowy double of the capital with its own arteries, squares, and crossroads. There are of course reminders of the *métro* subway and the sewage systems, but the subterranean galleries of the former quarries run much deeper, up to 20 to 25 metres below street level. It was precisely inside some of these galleries that the general ossuary of the city of Paris, which came to be known as the *Catacombes*, was established at the end of the 18th century. These

Parisian Catacombs were named after the Roman ones, even though Rome and Paris shared little else in common in this regard. Indeed, unlike the Catacombs of Rome, Naples and Syracuse, the Catacombs of Paris do not date back to the Greco-Roman period. Instead, they were the fruit of an administrative decision from the end of the Ancien Régime (Old Regime) period preceding the French Revolution. Nor were they ever used as a shelter for clandestine religious services or even as burial grounds—at least not direct burial grounds.

The Parisian Catacombs were established in the old limestone quarries of the Montrouge Plain, known as the quarries of the Tombe-Issoire[2]. In those times the site was located outside of Paris, which was still encircled by city walls: the Wall of the Farmers-General. It was not until 1860 when a vast annexing of towns in the Paris periphery took place that the capital achieved its current guise.

⬆ Sign indicating Tombe-Issoire, just at the exit of the Ossuary, but with the old spelling still visible: "Tombe Ysoire", with a single "s" and a "y" instead of the first "i".

2   It is interesting to note that the location elected for this new collective burial ground was none other than a spot designated in popular culture as the tomb of a legendary giant Isoré: the Tombe-Issoire.

➜ Underground quarry cross-section. Until the end of the 19ᵗʰ century, quarry workers would extract limestone blocks using a method like squirrels spinning a cage.

THE ANCIENT UNDERGROUND QUARRIES

Building materials were first excavated from the Paris subsoil during the Gallo-Roman times, from open quarries. It was not until the very end of the 12ᵗʰ century that extraction took place via underground digging which offered two benefits. Firstly, there was no more need to clear away the increasingly thick upper strata of soil; secondly, the top soil that was indispensable to crop farming could thus be preserved.

The first underground quarries, exploited as extensions of the open quarries, were located in the city suburbs. However, Paris continued to grow, overflowing each of the successive series of walls built to surround it. As the abandoned underground quarries fell into oblivion, houses were progressively built above them. At the same time, new galleries were being dug further out in the city's periphery. In his *Traité des pierres* (Treatise on Stones), Bernard de Palissy recalls his visit to the quarries of the Faubourg Saint-Marcel (in the present-day 13ᵗʰ arrondissement) in 1575, walking "for over one league" without seeing the light of day[3].

---

3 Bernard de Palissy, *Discours admirables de la nature des eaux et fontaines, tant naturelles qu'artificielles, des métaux, des sels et salines, des pierres, des terres, du feu et des émaux...*, Paris, Martin le Jeune, 1580, p.202.

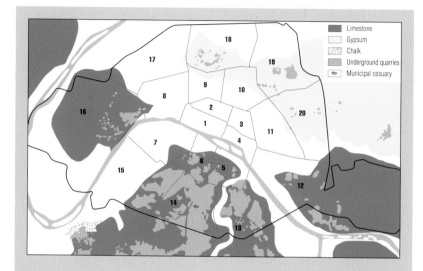

Quarry exploitation zones

Today, the areas of Paris undercut by the former limestone (or "Paris stone") quarries are located in the 5th, 6th, 12th, 13th, 14th, 15th and 16th *arrondissements*. The extraction zones are located under the small Parisian hills of Montparnasse, Montsouris, Montrouge, the Butte aux Cailles and the Colline de Chaillot (*mont, butte* and *colline* are French words for "hill"). Added to these are the 65 hectares of gypsum ("plaster of Paris") quarries in the 18th, 19th and 20th *arrondissements*, more precisely in the Ménilmontant, Montmartre and Buttes-Chaumont areas on the Right Bank of Paris. Altogether, this represents one tenth of the capital's surface area.

CONSOLIDATING THE QUARRIES

Since a portion of Paris was built above the void spaces of the ancient quarries, Parisians were soon reminded of their existence during the second half of the 18th century when several areas of the capital caved in. These cave-ins, technically known as subsidence sinkholes (*fontis* in French), varied in size, affecting both isolated houses and entire streets.

This hazard was described by Louis-Sébastien Mercier:
"All that you see aboveground comes precisely from the city's foundations, thus absent underground. Hence these terrifying concavities, which can be found under the houses of several areas of Paris, perched on the abyss. It would take no more than a slight impact to restore these stones to whence they once came at the cost of so much effort. [...] Envisaging this grand city as being shaped and sustained by such opposed means is food for thought indeed! These towers, these belfries, these temple arches tell the eye that what we see when we look up is that which is missing

↓ Masonry below a sinkhole stopped when Charles-Axel Guillaumot was General Quarry Inspector in Year 13 of the French Republic (September 1804 – August 1805).

from under our feet."[4] He went on to note: *"Reflecting on what a good portion of this magnificent town lies upon, one shudders secretly and begins to dread the action of centripetal force. [...] And one drinks, eats and sleeps in the very edifices resting upon this uncertain crust."*[5] In 1776, the King's State Council called on the services of Antoine Dupont, mathematician and geometer, to map the underground quarries and consolidate them by erecting pillars. However, the task at hand was so considerable that a department fully dedicated to this issue was created on 4 April 1777: the Inspection des Carrières sous Paris et Plaines Adjacentes (Inspection Unit for Quarries Below Paris and Surrounding Plains). It was placed under the direction of one of the King's architects, Charles-Axel Guillaumot, who held this position until his death in 1807. In this capacity, Guillaumot would become the "Man Who Saved Paris"[6]!

⬆ Portrait of the man who truly saved Paris: Charles-Axel Guillaumot (1730–1807), Grand Prix de Rome d'Architecture (1750), the King's First Architect.

Guillaumot organised the Quarry Inspection Unit, which still exists today (under the name "Inspection Générale des Carrières") and is now housed in the eastern pavilion of the Barrière d'Enfer (literally, the "Toll Gate of Hell"), where visitors line up to visit the Catacombs Museum. As if a sign of destiny, on the very day Guillaumot took up this position, a house on the Rue d'Enfer collapsed into an old quarry 20 metres below the Parisian pavement level.

---

4   Louis-Sébastien Mercier, *Tableau de Paris*, 12 volumes published between 1782 and 1788. Reprinted in Louis-Sébastien Mercier and Nicolas Restif de la Bretonne, *Paris le jour, Paris la nuit*, Paris, Robert Laffont, 1990, vol. 1, chapter 6 *"Les carrières"*, p.36.
5   *Ibid.*, vol. 2, chapter 189 *"Plancher d'une partie de la capitale"*, p.110.
6   As appropriately coined by Graham Robb (title of Chapter 3) in Graham Robb, *Parisians: An Adventure History of Paris*, New York, Picador, 2010.

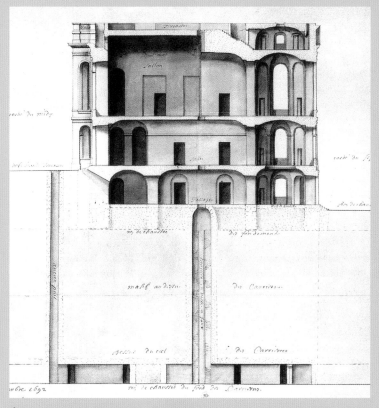

⬆ Cross-section of the Paris Observatory (F. d'Orbay, 1692). Constructed to study the celestial vault, the Observatory was built above another roof, that of the underground quarries.

Consolidations below the observatory

Before the creation of the Quarry Inspection Unit, a few prestigious estates had already been selectively consolidated when they had threatened to collapse into the quarry voids on which they had been built. This was the case of the Charterhouse of the Carthusian Order in 1259, as well as the Val-de-Grâce during its construction in 1645, the Capuchin monastery in 1653 (under the present-day Cochin Hospital), and the Observatoire during its building in 1672.

Charles-Axel Guillaumot introduced a quarry consolidation policy in response to the French Civil Code stipulating that "underground ownership stems from land ownership"[7].

As the Quarry Inspection Unit was subject to the King's authority, Guillaumot had to safeguard public roads and the King's properties by erecting pillars from the bottom of quarries to their roofs to act as retrospectively created foundations for the edifices built on the surface. Every street located in an undercut area was thus doubled by a gallery following the same layout, hence enabling the evolution of voids to be monitored.

These galleries had to be sufficiently large to allow a man to stand and pass through with a wheelbarrow: *"To monitor the preservation of these constructions at all times, it was necessary to render them accessible; to this effect, a gallery wide enough to allow passage of construction materials was left under and within the public way; at the gallery's farthest point, another wall was built. Perpendicular galleries were dug here and there to enable commu-*

nication between both sides of the public way and to allow movement from one gallery to the next."[8]

This is how Paris came to develop an underground double of its eighteenth-century aboveground topography. Incidentally, the galleries—developed over 150 linear kilometres—were magnificently mapped by the geometer-topographers of the Quarry Inspection Unit from the onset of its creation.

It is through galleries like these that visitors pass through from the entrance staircase to the vestibule of the Catacombs, and then from the Ossuary exit to the exit staircase.

THE SAINTS-INNOCENTS CEMETERY

The Saints-Innocents Cemetery —the first to be transferred to the new Tombe-Issoire Ossuary— had hosted for over ten centuries the remains of parishioners from Paris' twenty-two parishes[9], as well as cadavers from the morgue and numerous deceased from the

---

7   Article 552 of the Civil Code, reference no. 1804-01-27 promulgated on 6 February 1804.

8   Charles-Axel Guillaumot, *Mémoire sur les travaux ordonnés dans les carrières sous Paris, et plaines adjacentes*, Paris, 1797, p.11.
9   In 1572, the Protestant victims of the Saint-Bartholomew Massacre were also laid to rest there.

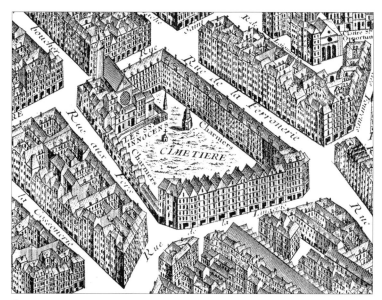

⬆ General view of Saints-Innocents
Cemetery, on Turgot's map of Paris in 1734.

Hôtel-Dieu[10]. Louis-Sébastien Mercier reports that the *"Hôtel-Dieu has all it takes to be pestilential, because of its damp and unventilated atmosphere; wounds turn gangrenous more easily, and both scurvy and scabies wreak havoc when patients sojourn there. What in theory are the most innocuous diseases rapidly acquire serious complications by way of the contaminated air; for that precise reason, simple head and leg wounds become lethal in that hospital.*
Nothing proves my point so well as the tally of patients who perish miserably each year in the Paris Hôtel-Dieu and in the Bicêtre Hôtel-Dieu; a fifth of the patients succumb; a frightful tally treated only with the greatest indifference!"[11]

---

10 Hôtel-Dieu (literally, "hostel of God") was the name given to the main hospital in French towns.

11 L.-S. Mercier, *op. cit.*, vol. 3, chapter 269, *"L'Hôtel-Dieu"*, p.139.

At the edges of the Saints-Innocents Cemetery, charnel houses of wide proportions sheltered the human remains that were exhumed as new graves were being dug. Mercier adds: *"Beneath these mass graves, which strike the greatest terror in the universe when glimpsed, rats live among the human bones, disturbing and lifting them, seeming to*

↑ A charnel house-ossuary in the Saints-Innocents slum; the stacking of bones in the Catacombs would follow in the same fashion.

animate the dead as they indicate to the present generation the ranks among which they will soon stand: here, the debris of humanity is placed, not according to past rank, but to physical size. They will soon all turn to chalky earth."[12]

While bones were stacked in a conspicuously decorative fashion, corpses rotting in the ground poisoned the air. Those residing near the Saints-Innocents as well as other cemeteries were the first to suffer from this insalubrity: *"The stench of cadavers could be smelt in almost all churches; [...] the reek of putrefaction continued to poison the faithful."*[13] The generous use of incense inside the churches did not suffice to mask the foul stink. On 17 July 1793, a petition demanded that another location be found for the cemetery of Ville-l'Évêque (where Louis XVI and Marie-Antoinette were buried) as the fetor of rotting cadavers became unbearable for neighbouring citizens as well as a danger to the City of Paris.

Complaints from Parisians living in the vicinity of cemeteries compounded those that had been formulated as early as the 16th century by doctors regarding the unhealthiness of the Saints-Innocents. In houses close to the cemetery, broth and milk went sour in the space of a few hours, wine turned to vinegar, and merely resting one's hand on the walls soaked with a deadly dampness was a foolhardy act.

12 L.-S. Mercier, *op. cit.*, vol. 5, chapter 422 *"Les rats"*, p.190.

13 *Ibid.*, vol. 1, chapter 43 *"L'air vicié"*, p.49.

The accumulation of cadavers had elevated the level of the cemetery ground by nearly two and a half metres. Mass graves could contain 1,200 to 1,500 corpses, while private burials amounted to less than 200 per year. The last gravedigger from that era, François Pourrain, estimated that close to 90,000 bodies had been buried in the Saints-Innocents in less than thirty years. In 1779, a mass grave destined to hold over 2,000 corpses was dug, and a few months later, in February 1780, the walls of a basement on the Rue de la Lingerie, adjacent to the cemetery, collapsed under the sheer weight of bodies. Without further delay, an injunction forbidding use of the cemetery was issued and the

⬆ Under the Montsouris Plain, now part of the 14th *arrondissement*.

Prefect of Police Lenoir considered the possibility of transferring the bones to the old quarries of the Montsouris Plain. His successor Thiroux de Crosne[14], General Lieutenant of Police in Paris from 1785 to 1789 pursued the idea by ordering General Quarry Inspector Charles-Axel Guillaumot to prepare the location for this purpose. On the site of the Saints-Innocents Cemetery, a vegetable and herb market was to be set up.

---

14   During the French Revolution, he went into exile in England for some time. Upon his return to Paris, he was executed on 28 April 1794. His predecessor, Lenoir, also fled the Revolution from 1790 to 1802, going first to Switzerland, then Vienna.

THE CLOSING
OF THE CEMETERY

The State Council ruled on 9 November 1785 that the Saints-Innocents Cemetery would officially be closed, evacuated and converted into the public market it has remained to this day—now known as the Forum des Halles. Following this ruling, Monseigneur Leclerc de Juigné, Archbishop of Paris, issued a decree on 16 November 1786, ordering *"the removal of the Saints-Innocents Cemetery, its demolition and its evacuation, entailing the turning of the soil to a depth of five feet and the sieving of earth, with any remaining corpses or bones to be transported and buried in the new underground cemetery of the Montrouge Plain."*[15]

Louis-Sébastien Mercier refers to the Saints-Innocents Cemetery after its closure and conversion into a market: *"We have men-*

15 Cited by Paul Fassy, *Les Catacombes, étude historique*, Paris, E. Dentu, 1861, p.33.

← The Catacombs Ossuary was established under what was once countryside that was part of the township of Montrouge (map by Delagrive, 1730–1740).

tioned that each year, nearly three thousand bodies were brought to the Saints-Innocents Cemetery, situated in the most populated district. The dead had been buried there since the time of Philippe le Bel. Ten million cadavers at the very least have dissolved in that narrow space. What a crucible! A market where vegetables and herbs are sold has risen from this human debris. I cannot walk through it without pondering. Oh, what stories would flow from these walls if only the dead could talk!"[16]
All this did not prevent the further—but temporary— burials of some of the 1830 combatants on the Saints-Innocents site. On 25 July 1830, the "Four Ordinances" of Charles X led to an uprising on the market place, which became a stage of skirmishes between the army and the rebels on 28 and 29 July. Approximately thirty victims were buried on the spot; for a few hours, the Saints-Innocents reverted to what the site had ceased to be for over forty years.

TRANSFERRING THE BONES TO THE CATACOMBS

On 7 April 1786, the grounds of the Tombe-Issoire were sanctified in the presence of the Abbots Mottret, Maillet and Asseline, the architects Legrand and Molinos, and Charles-Axel Guillaumot. Transportation of bones was scrupulously ritualised: at nightfall, funerary carts draped in black sheets, accompanied by torchbearers, followed by priests wearing surplices and stoles and chanting the Office of the Dead, would make their way to a service shaft to dispose of loads that one poet described as a *"shapeless debris-monument to the departed"*[17].

➜ A relatively well-preserved wall of bones transferred from Saint-Landry Cemetery in 1792, topped by a frieze of skulls.

16 L.-S. Mercier, *op. cit.*, vol. 9, chapter 752 *"Cimetière fermé"*, p.292.

17 *"Un informe débris monument du trépas"* in the original French poem by Gabriel-Marie-Jean-Baptiste Legouvé, *"La Mélancolie"*, in *Le Mérite des femmes et autres poésies*, Paris, Ant. Aug. Renouard, 1804, p.176.

The first transfers from the Saints-Innocents lasted fifteen months (with intermissions during hot weather); then, between 1792 and 1814, sixteen other cemeteries were eliminated. In total, the remains of two million Parisians were withdrawn from the Saints-Innocents during the successive exhumations needed

⬆ Nocturnal exhumation of bones from Saints-Innocents Cemetery (Watercolour by Jean-Nicolas Sobre, 1750–1799, Musée Carnavalet).

to fully empty the cemetery. It was thus from 1786 to 1814 that cemeteries adjoining churches were similarly emptied and the dead moved to their new underground "haven of peace".

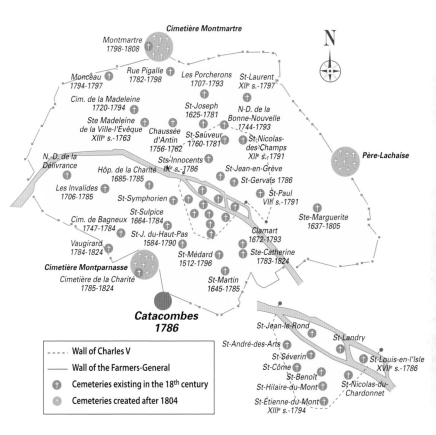

↑ Locations of the main cemeteries transferred to the Catacombs Ossuary before 1860. The three newly created Parisian cemeteries were found outside the Wall of the Farmers-General – as well as the Catacombs.

Paris had sundry burial grounds: in the 13th century, there were five public cemeteries (the Saints-Innocents, Saint-Benoît, Saint-Honoré, Saint-Landry and Saint-Nicolas des Champs), and in the 16th century, there were sixty-five churches and chapels each with adjoining cemeteries or interior crypts. In the 17th century, there were 4 abbeys for men, 42 convents for men, 12 seminaries, 8 abbeys for women, 44 convents for women, 15 religious communities, around 50 parishes, 10 parish churches, 80 chapels

⬆ Bone stacking, according to a photo by Nadar; a scene similar to what could be seen in the 18th century (*Le Monde illustré*, 1865).

from the ground, be instantly placed in empty vats of Roman cement and thus carried to n°6, Rue de Vaugirard [marked by the inscription "Ossuary of the West" in the Catacombs Ossuary] *pending their final inhumation in the Catacombs"*[18]. The Vaugirard Cemetery was emptied from September 1859 onwards and the remains transferred to the Catacombs. A new tour itinerary was then established so that visitors start by discovering the latest bone additions.

⬆ Characteristic decor in the Catacombs Ossuary, according to a photograph by Nadar (in *Les Catacombes de Paris*, prefaced by Monsieur de Cormenin, 1862).

and 20 chapters, almost all of which held burial grounds. Added to these were fifteen public cemeteries on top of the Saints-Innocents, as well as two cemeteries exclusively reserved for Israelites and another two for Protestants.

The Ossuary of the Catacombs was enlarged for the last time in 1859–1860, as Baron Haussmann's extensive remodelling of Paris uncovered forgotten cemeteries, each adding their share of human remains. Special measures were taken to ensure that *"the bones, upon their extraction*

---

18 Fassy, *op. cit.*, p.27

The Ossuary ceiling, like a stone palimpsest, reveals the changes in itinerary since the creation of the Catacombs.

OSSEMENTS
DES YNNOC
EN AVRII

Most notable inscription referring to the original transfers of bones from the "Ynnocents" (*sic*), but not accessible to visitors; we can see two tears of mourning on either side of the cross.

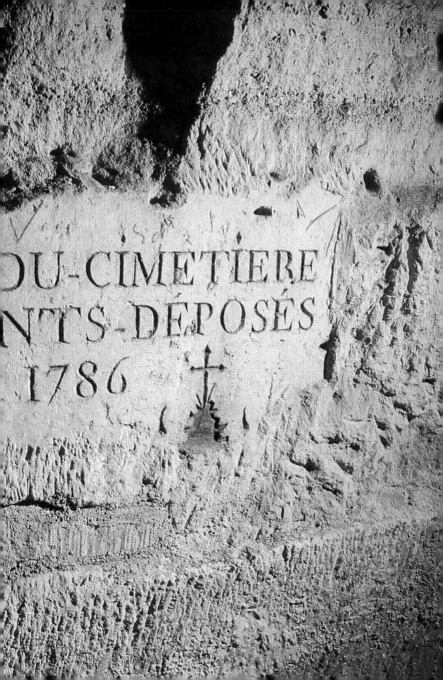

OSSEMENTS DE L'A
CIMETIÈRE DE LA MA
(RUE DE LA VILLE LÉVÊ
DÉPOSÉS EN 1844 DANS
DE L'OUEST ET TRANSFÉ
CATACOMBES EN SEPT

Ossuary maintenance once consisted in replacing skulls that had "mysteriously" disappeared. This is no longer done.

Parisian cemeteries transferred to the Catacombs

The following long list enumerates the different bone deposits—in the order in which they are found along the Ossuary itinerary—and mentions the date of their arrival at the Tombe-Issoire. It is worth mentioning that it would be impossible to guarantee the actual presence of the remains of celebrities previously buried in old Parisian cemeteries at the spots indicated as their burial sites by memorial stones. On top of this, the walls of bones were not always restored faithfully.

↑ Bones from Saint-Esprit Cemetery at the former entrance, a gallery now closed to the public.

- Saint-Nicolas des Champs (1859)
- Saint-Laurent (1859)
- Saint-Jacques du Haut-Pas (1859)
- Former leper hospital, Rue de Douai (1859)
- Saint-Jean, Rue du Faubourg Montmartre (1859)
- Trinité and Saint-Leu (1859).

In 1906, new remains were uncovered during the construction works of the *métro* subway line near the Boulevard de Sébastopol.

- Trinité Cemetery (1859)
- Trinité Hospital, Rue Saint-Denis and Rue Greneta (1814)
- Couvent des Carmes (Carmelite convent), Place Maubert (1814)
- Saint-Landry (1792)
- Saints-Innocents Cemetery (1786) and eight further deposits (from 1786 to 1809). On 13 June 1786, Madame de Mailly's coffin was brought to the Tombe-Issoire. She had been one of Louis XV's numerous mistresses.
- Saint-Étienne des Grès (1787)
- Saint-Laurent (1804)
- Blancs-Manteaux Church and Cloister (1804)
- Petit Saint-Antoine Church and Cloister (1804)

Saint-Eustache (1787), where Colbert, Minister of State, had been laid to rest.

Sainte-Croix de la Bretonnerie (1793)

Saint-André des Arts (1794)

A further deposit from the Petit Saint-Antoine Church and Cloister (1804)

Cemetery adjoining the Saint-Jacques de la Boucherie Tower (1859)

Madeleine Cemetery, Rue de la Ville l'Évêque (1859). Burial grounds for approximately 1,000 Swiss Guards killed at the Tuileries, as well as 1,343 people —including Charlotte Corday— executed at the Carrousel or on Place Louis XV (the present-day Place de la Concorde) between 26 August 1782 and 13 June 1794.

Vaugirard Cemetery (1859)

Saint-Jean de l'Hôtel de Ville (1804)

Another deposit from Sainte-Croix de la Bretonnerie (1793)

Capucins Saint-Honoré Church and Cloister (1804). The martyr Saint-Ovidius was buried there. Initially been laid to rest in the Catacombs of Rome, his remains were brought back to France by Pope Alexander VII. This makes him the only person to have been buried in two of the world's most famous catacombs. Louvois, State Secretary of War under Louis XIV, as well as Madame de Pompadour, were also buried at the Capucins.

Saint-Esprit (1804)

Saint-Laurent (1804)

Other deposits are invisible to the visitor, in the Catacombes Basses (Lower Catacombs) or elsewhere: Saint-Nicolas des Champs (1804), a further deposit from Saint-Landry (1792), Saint-André des Arts (1794), Capucins Saint-Honoré Church and Cloister (1804), the small cemetery on Saint-Louis Island (1811)…

⬆ In the Lower Catacombs, closed to the public; above the sign, only the skull on the left still clings on pathetically; the rest have vanished.

← Amongst the first bones seen by visitors are those from Saint-Jacques du Haut-Pas Church.

↓ One of the different signs indicating bones from Saints-Innocents Cemetery, during the very first transfer in 1786.

↑ Sign once indicating bones from Bernardins church, today on the floor close to the inaccessible former Mineralogy Collection Cabinet

← Signs from the period 1859–1860 were no longer simple rectangular plates as those engraved in Héricart de Thury's time, but had a unique shape, whether they indicated the origins of bones or bore quotations. Here, indicating bones from two former cemeteries, Trinité Hospital and Saint-Leu Saint-Gilles Church.

Only the largest and most significant bone transfers to the Catacombs were recorded in writing. Many deposits occurred before 1859. For instance, in July 1847 and in August 1853, the Filles de la Charité (Daughters of Charity, also known as the *sœurs grises*, literally, "grey sisters") Convent brought its contingent of bones; and in May 1853, remains from the Maison des Prêtres de la Mission de Saint-Lazare were also added. Bone transfers from Saint-Sépulchre Church occurred in 1786, 1787, 1808, and again in July 1856.

Furthermore, in 1878, the remains of a group of Communards uncovered on Rue de Phalsbourg during archaeological excavations were transferred to the Catacombs. The extension of the Palais Brongniart on Place de la Bourse in 1902 revealed some bones, also transferred there. Bones from the East Cemetery (Père-Lachaise) were also conveyed to the Tombe-Issoire in December 1933. In 1947, bones found in various Parisian archaeological digging sites were still redirected to the Ossuary, although these dispatches had by then become considerably less voluminous.

From 1911, a specific location was reserved in the Père-Lachaise Cemetery for housing historical sepulchres uncovered during excavations: a concession on Avenue Circulaire (79th Division), near the disused Petite Ceinture railroad tunnel, adjacent to the Gambetta public garden. However, it was not until 1925 that human remains uncovered at Port-Royal—probably those of two nuns from the Abbey—were buried there for the first time.

From December 1973 to February 1974, during preparatory digs preliminary to renovations to the Forum des Halles (when the old Halles markets were being moved to Rungis) and development of the RER train station, some thirty Merovingian sarcophagi were dug up and other bones found and collected.

⬇ This sign, now gone, identified a bone transfer dating from 1933, thus long after the last known transfers in 1860.

OSSEMENTS PROVENANT DU CIMETIÈRE DE L'EST
DÉCEMBRE 1933

MONTPARNASSE CEMETERY

Montparnasse Cemetery constitutes an exception. In the course of urban improvement works in its vicinity (including the creation of the Rue Émile Richard which now splits the cemetery in two), large quantities of bones were found and transferred to the municipal ossuary. However, after 1870, following the destruction of the cemetery's old mass graves — and since it was not possible to enlarge the Catacombs any further —, a huge quantity of bones was placed under Montparnasse Cemetery itself, within disused quarry galleries previously converted for that purpose.

In 1895, more remains were discovered near Rue du Champ-d'Asile (the present-day Rue Froidevaux). It is hypothesized that these were the cholera victims of 1832 (out of 700,000 inhabitants, Paris counted 100,000 victims). These remains were transferred to the quarries below the cemetery and laid to rest there in no specific order. This mass grave, measuring close to 300 square metres, is situated at a depth of roughly twenty metres below the pavement level

⬆ To fill the ossuaries under Montparnasse Cemetery, the same method was used as at the Catacombs: bones were unloaded by service shafts.

(six spaces like this one exist beneath Montparnasse cemetery). In November 1922, further remains uncovered in the vicinity during urban electricity works were relocated to the Catacombs.

It is unlikely that these bones will be seen by visitors to the Catacombs, for they lay in one of the ossuaries under Montparnasse Cemetery, another spot where bones were heaped.

THE VISITOR'S
ITINERARY

On the roofs of galleries leading to the
Ossuary, at strategic intersections,
inscriptions such as this one (outside
today's itinerary) could be seen.

The Visitor's Itinerary

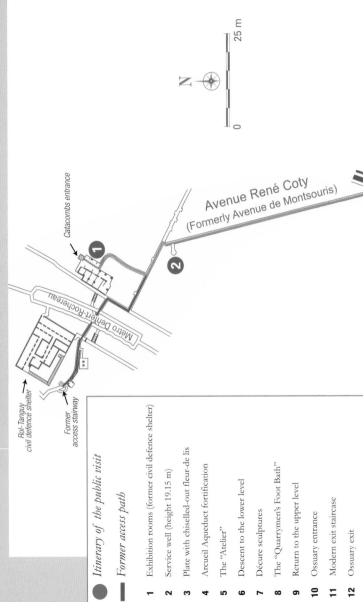

- Itinerary of the public visit
- Former access path

1 Exhibition rooms (former civil defence shelter)
2 Service well (height 19.15 m)
3 Plate with chiselled-out fleur-de lis
4 Arcueil Aqueduct fortification
5 The "Atelier"
6 Descent to the lower level
7 Décure sculptures
8 The "Quarrymen's Foot Bath"
9 Return to the upper level
10 Ossuary entrance
11 Modern exit staircase
12 Ossuary exit
13 Pedagogical *fontis* (sinkholes)

Catacombs entrance

Rol-Tanguy
civil defence shelter

Former
access stairway

Metro Denfert-Rochereau

Avenue René Coty
(Formerly Avenue de Montsouris)

N

0   25 m

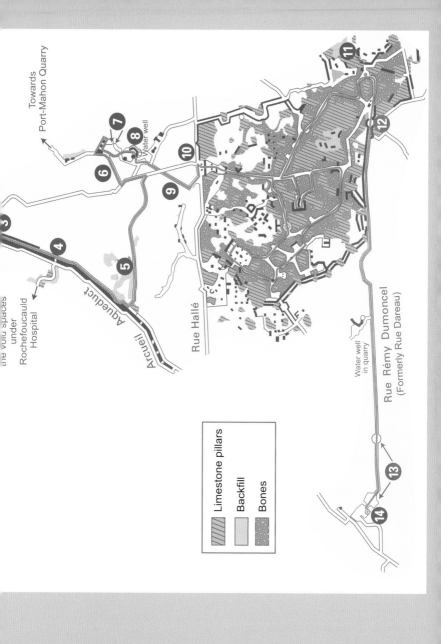

Towards
Port-Mahon Quarry

Water well

The void spaces
under
Rochefoucauld
Hospital

Aqueduct

Arcueil

Rue Hallé

Water well
in quarry

Rue Rémy Dumoncel
(Formerly Rue Dareau)

Limestone pillars

Backfill

Bones

↑ The entrance to the Catacombs is on the left of this former tollgate building, *"Inspection Générale des Carrières de Paris et du Département de la Seine"*.

Since the beginning of the 1980s, visitors have accessed the Catacombs via the eastern pavilion of the wall built by Claude Nicolas Ledoux from 1784 onwards. This wall was not meant to protect the city from potential enemies but to fight tax evasion. All food and merchandise entering Paris were subject to a tax. Before the wall was erected, the *octroi* (a city toll, the modern equivalent of which would be an excise tax) was signalled by a wooden fence with openings in certain spots allowing tax evaders to enter the city unnoticed by officials. To remedy this situation, unfavourable for the Treasury, the Ferme Générale (the Farmers-General tax-farming operation whose role has now been taken over by the Ministry of Finance) requested the erection of an impenetrable wall pierced by gates that could not be circumvented. Claude Nicolas Ledoux thus built *"a barrier barring Paris making Paris broody"*[19]. Of this wall, only four gates remain today out of the fifty-four that existed then. The path of this wall, which defined the Paris city limits until

1860, can still be observed today by taking a look at the routes of the two over-ground *métro* lines: line 2 (Nation to Place Charles-de-Gaulle-Étoile via Barbès-Rochechouart) and line 6 (Nation to Place Charles-de-Gaulle-Étoile via Denfert-Rochereau). Besides the Barrière d'Enfer (or "Toll Gate of Hell", also known as the Orléans Toll Gate) on the Place Denfert-Rochereau, the only remaining vestiges of the city toll walls are the buildings that can be seen on Place de la Nation (the Barrière du Trône, literally the "Toll Gate of the Throne"), Place de Stalingrad (La Villette Rotunda) as well as the Monceau Park Rotunda. On 1 January 1860, the wall was demolished and Paris fiscal limits enlarged: until right after the Second World War, these

---

19   Popular eighteenth-century Parisian alliterative expression, sometimes attributed to Beaumarchais. In French: *"Mur murant Paris rendant Paris murmurant"*.

limits were to be found where the Périphérique (Paris ring road) is now situated.

Paris's annexing, in 1860, of the peripheral towns surrounding it had the unforeseen consequence of integrating to the capital three great burial sites that had initially been specifically created to exist outside the city limits: the Eastern Cemetery (Père-Lachaise, dating back to 1804), the Southern Cemetery (Montparnasse, established in 1824) and the Northern Cemetery (Montmartre, created in 1825). The same was true for the Catacombs, which originally belonged to the town of Montrouge before it was annexed to Paris.

THE ENTRANCE

In the past, the entrance was found in the courtyard of the western pavilion of the Barrière d'Enfer. After opening up access with a puzzle lock, the guide would lead visitors down a 90-step staircase. The group would then walk beneath the Place Denfert-Rochereau, just under the line 4 *métro* station, which was signalled by an enamel street plate. It was not until the beginning of the 1980s that the current access was created.

⬇ Place Denfert-Rochereau, 1935. Candle-holding visitors patiently wait in the courtyard of the former entrance; at the time, visits were rare.

⬆ To open the access door, guides would use puzzle lock like this one.

⬇ From the former access, visitors passing under Denfert-Rochereau *métro* station would see this sign indicating reinforcing works.

CHEMIN DE FER MÉTROPOLITAIN MUNICIPAL
LIGNE N° 4

CONSOLIDATION des ANCIENNES CARRIÈRES 2ᵉ Lot

Travaux Exécutés en 1   1905

M. WICKERSHEIMER _ Ingé   r e   f des Mines
M. WEISS   _   Ingénieur des Mines
M.M. GERA DS & VA   T _ Sous-Inspecteurs Municipaux
M. VIVO   _   Chef de Subdivision
Mᵣ JOYEUX Entrepreneur

Under the First French Empire, tour guides were free to choose the path they preferred. Visitors had to apply for visiting permission from the Catacombs head office, then located on Rue Saint-Dominique (now renamed Rue Royer-Collard, in the 5th *arrondissement*). The number of visitors was already impressive; this led to damage, lost visitors and miscellaneous abuses, prompting the closure of the Catacombs in 1830. The Mayor of Montrouge—the Catacombs were attached to this town until 1860—implored the Prefect of Paris Rambuteau to re-open the Ossuary to the public. His request was rejected: *"It is my*

A former strategic intersection: the visitor could turn left at the pillar towards Port-Mahon and Décure's sculptures, or right to head straight to the Ossuary.

opinion that to expose in such a fashion these piles of bones, arranged according to an entirely unseemly symmetry, would amount to a profanation. Offering such a spectacle to the public's curiosity could be construed of as immoral and wholly unworthy of a civilized people."[20] Group visits were authorized again a few years later, but were limited to four per year. In 1867, visits began to take place on a monthly rhythm, and after 1874, bimonthly. Today, the Catacombs are open to the public every day except Mondays and public holidays.

THE CIVIL DEFENCE SHELTER

A 131-step staircase has been built to replace the original one created by Guillaumot in 1799. When taking the former entrance, visitors going under the Place Denfert-Rochereau would walk alongside the civil defence shelter from which Colonel Rol-Tanguy coordinated the Paris uprising from 19 to 25 August 1944, by urging the population to stand up against Nazi occupants.

The new entrance leads to a landing at the bottom of the first 25 steps (a means to skirt around a *métro* gallery discovered "by chance" during construction

---

20 É. Gérards, *op. cit.*, p.463.

⬆ The shelter from which the Paris uprising was commanded from 19 to 25 August 1944, to chase Nazis from the capital.

built everywhere underneath the city as places of refuge during aerial attacks using poison gases, which had been discovered and used during the First World War. In 1937, a section of the Paris International Exposition was devoted to different types of individual or collective shelters. Voids such as those provided by disused quarries, the *métro* or even basements were thus used as shelters, as were sewers and aqueducts, although more rarely. The advantage of the former quarries was their considerable depth: at twenty or so metres below street level, they offered adequate protection against all types of bombs.

THE GALLERIES

To prevent nineteenth-century visitors from losing their way in the galleries adjacent to those of the Ossuary, a black tar line was traced on the gallery ceilings to mark the path they should follow. The location of this marking can be explained by the fact that visitors lit their way using candles or tapers (electricity was not installed until 1974), which they held high. This "lifeline" was consequently drawn where it could best be seen.

works!) and then opens onto two small rooms used for exhibitions. This spot is a small portion of another civil defence shelter. Indeed, numerous shelters were created at the outbreak of the Second World War, many of which still exist today.

The deterioration of international relations and "the noise of marching boots" in the beginning of the 1930s were an incentive to pass laws organizing civil defence. Before the end of the decade, shelters were

↑ Long access corridor. To allow enough space for a person to stand upright, workers had to dig over this gallery crossing an old mining site using the *hagues et bourrages* technique.

"We etched a broad black line commencing at the base of the staircase and meandering all the way through this vast labyrinth. A stray visitor, provided he has light, need only follow this Ariadne's thread to find the door. From place to place, the line bears an arrow pointing towards the exit door, as the flow of a river is marked on a map."[21]

21 L. F. Hivert, *Esquisse sur les catacombes de Paris et sur les catacombes de Rome, la montagne Montmartre et le mont Valérien*, Paris, A. Hivert, 1860, p.8.

The gallery at the end of the shelter / exhibition room is as recent as the staircase; the black line is only visible when one reaches the path served by the former entrance. Today, this marking is no longer a necessity since it is not possible to wander out of the Ossuary zone anymore: walls at least a dozen metres thick confine the site (which stretches over roughly 1.5 kilometres, 600 metres of which are dedicated to the Ossuary) and isolate it from the rest of the network of underground quarries.

⬆ Numbering of the 75th consolidation pillar erected in 1780 when Charles-Axel Guillaumot was General Quarry Inspector.

INSCRIPTIONS

In the galleries leading to the Ossuary, two types of engraved inscriptions can be seen on the gallery walls: engraved street names (or engravings indicating locations), and more enigmatic inscriptions, for instance

⬇ Indicating Avenue de Montsouris (today Avenue René-Coty) overhead.

42 J 1847 — the first that can be observed on the path, giving a precise indication of the date of consolidation works. In this case, the inscription means that we are facing the 42nd retaining pillar, erected under the supervision of General Quarry Inspector Juncker (hence the initial "J"), in service from 1842 to 1851. To facilitate the deciphering of similar markings, here, in chronological order, is a list of General Inspectors, limited to those whose initials can be encountered on the path:

■ "**G**" for Guillaumot, Inspector from 1777 to 1807 (his service was interrupted during the Revolution, during which he was

⬆ Not all "G"s indicate Guillaumot. In 1878, it was Ernest Gentil who was General Quarry Inspector. Sign with a correction: 85 turned into 87.

⬆ Consolidation work under Paul Weiss: the last known engraved date. Weiss located, in 1905, the remains of J.-P. Jones, a hero of the American War of Independence.

imprisoned for many months)
- ■ "**B**" (or "B2") for Bralle, who replaced Guillaumot during the Revolution
- ■ "**J**" for Juncker, Inspector from 1842 to 1851
- ■ "**D**" for Descottes, Inspector from 1872 to 1875
- ■ "**T**" for Tournaire, Inspector from 1875 to 1878
- ▨ Another "**G**" for Gentil, Inspector from 1878 to 1879
- ■ "**K**" for Keller, Inspector from 1885 to 1896 (these markings can be found after leaving the Ossuary, in the exit gallery)
- ■ "**W**" for Weiss (1907 to 1911), whose monogram, dated 1909, only appears once on a pillar at the entrance of the Ossuary.

It is worth mentioning that Inspector Héricart de Thury (Inspector from 1809 to 1831) was responsible for the creation of most of the monuments that can be found in the Ossuary as well as for the opening of the site to the public. His works in the quarry galleries are signalled by the ligature "HT" (the second vertical bar of the H coincides with that of the T). However, none of the consolidations erected during his service are visible on the visitors' path. Plates indicating locations enabled employees of the Quarry Inspection Unit to always locate themselves in relation to the streets above and to find their bearings. They are genuine street

Misleading inscriptions

In the Ossuary, the inscription "*7bre*" can sometimes be read on plates identifying bone deposits. This etymological abbreviation designates the month of September, although it is actually the ninth month of the year (thus, "*8bre*" stands for October, "*9bre*" for November, and "*10bre*" for December). This is the consequence of a calendar revision dating back to August 1564 under King Charles IX, who imposed January as the first month of the year. This measure was effective from the 1 January 1567, hence pushing back the calendar by two months.

⬇ Bones from the Small Cemetery of île Saint-Louis are no longer maintained as they are in a gallery not viewed by the public..

plates, identical to those that first appeared in the capital around 1728–1729. This system was adopted from 1777 onwards in the underground quarries and was never changed, so that today's visitors can explore a true museum of the topography of Paris, frozen in the Enlightenment age.

In addition to the hard limestone street plates embedded in the quarry walls (similar to the ones in the streets of Paris), inscriptions encountered underground were sometimes also directly engraved onto gallery walls, or onto free stones integrated into pillars.

⬆ *Regard 25* of the Arcueil Aqueduct, in the gardens of La Rochefoucauld Hospital.

THE ARCUEIL AQUEDUCT

All the galleries that the visitor walks through before reaching the Ossuary are surveillance galleries of the Quarry Inspection Unit, situated directly below road surfaces, with the exception of one, built under a water way: the Arcueil Aqueduct.

Since its birth, Paris has drawn its main water supply from the River Seine or from wells. Distribution of spring water to the capital was only organized for short periods of time and represented but a small fraction of the volumes that were consumed.

The first city water catchments were built by the Romans near the present-day town of Rungis (12 kilometres southeast of Paris), but only to supply the palace of the Thermes de Cluny (thermal baths). Back then, water was brought by a duct roughly 16 kilometres long; however, this only lasted until the 9th century. In the Middle Ages, from the 12th century onwards, a few springs were drained on the slopes of Belleville and the Pré-Saint-Gervais (northeast districts of Paris). It was not until the 17th century that new city water catchments were set up, again in the vicinity of Rungis. Foundations of the Arcueil Aqueduct, built from 1613 to 1623, can be glimpsed by Catacomb visitors. The course of this aqueduct

⬆ On the path towards the Ossuary, the gallery at one point runs underneath the Arcueil Aqueduct.

was punctuated by 27 *regards*[22] enabling the authorities to access the aqueduct to check its working condition and, more to the point, to verify whether water was being clandestinely diverted. The exploitation of underground quarries in the proximity of roads and aqueducts[23] or underneath a neighbour's property was forbidden by Law; nevertheless, many abuses were reported, and the Arcueil Aqueduct was no exception. When Guillaumot took up his post in 1777, he soon discovered that, here and there, the aqueduct rested on quarry voids responsible for numerous leaks. Masonry works right below the aqueduct succeeded in consolidating the structure; they are visible when walking along Avenue de Montsouris to the "Atelier", with a double system of surveillance galleries on either side. Since 1860, the year when Avenue Reille was created, interrupting the course of the aqueduct, water has stopped flowing through that portion of the aqueduct.

---

22   The French word *regard* designates a small stone edifice built above an aqueduct, used for service access and constituting an urban equivalent to the country springhouse.

23   It was forbidden to exploit quarries located less than 15 fathoms (28 metres) from main roads, fountain ducts and other public structures; infringements were punishable by fines and corporal punishment.

THE FRENCH REVOLUTION

The French Revolution left its imprint in the quarries below Paris on plates marking locations or consolidation works. 22 September 1792 was proclaimed the first day of Year I of the Republic according to the new calendar, which was to last only 14 years. The Quarry Inspection Unit was a scrupulous and rigorous administration: dates marking consolidation works were engraved in the limestone following this new calendar from 2 R to 14 R; despite the insurgency above ground, works continued undisturbed.

Thus, in the galleries leading to the Ossuary, we can read the following inscriptions: 3 G 13 R (third pillar of the consolidation works by Guillaumot on Year XIII of the Republic), 1 B 4 R (first portion of works directed by Bralle—who replaced Guillaumot when he was imprisoned in Versailles—on Year IV of the Republic) or 5 B² 4 R. To indicate religious premises situated above the circulation galleries of the Quarry Inspection Unit, the latter had affixed fleur-de-lis on plates marking their

⬇ Consolidation under Bralle, in Year 4 of the French Republic, while Guillaumot was imprisoned.

↑ At the top two corners of this sign, the fleurs-de-lis were erased in 1793, exactly ten years after they were engraved.

près l'Hospice la Charité" (*Regard* n°25 near the Charity Hospice) were chiselled out, whereas the fleur-de-lis are still visible on a similar plate located on the other side of the present-day La Rochefoucauld Hospital and upon which the words "*Hospice des Pères de la Charité*" (Fathers of Charity Hospice) are engraved. The latter area was isolated from the large passageways used by workers, contrary to the "*Regard 25*" zone located on the public pathway of the Ossuary, which could not escape even the most distracted glance.

↓ Nearby, a sign with its fleurs-de-lis intact, as this sector was difficult to access at the time.

location. In 1793, a decree published by the Convention ordered that all symbols of royalty be removed from the public monuments of Paris; the fleur-de-lis inside the galleries were thus systematically erased. Nevertheless, a few examples fortunately survived the revolutionary furore, either because they were situated in places difficult to access during the Revolution, or because they were masked. This accounts for the fact that the two upper corners of the plate "*Regard 25*

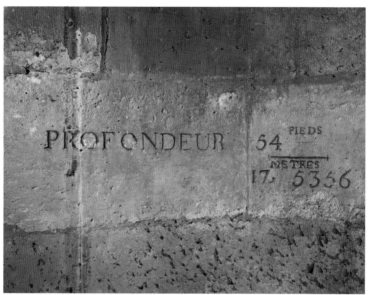

↑ Conversion of inch-feet measurements to the newly created, but not entirely assimilated, metric system.

Besides the creation of the Republican calendar, the French Revolution is also responsible for the invention of the metric system. Before 1795, the inch-feet system was in use, with many regional variations. The metre — created to establish a common and stable measure — was defined as *"the ten-millionth part of the quadrant of a meridian"* according to calculations by Méchain and Cassini. This new measure of length, defined from a purely mathematical standpoint, had the unforeseen consequence of making workers lose their bearings: accustomed as they were to measures based on corporal lengths, they failed to understand the relative importance of submultiples. Consequently, when it became necessary to convert Quarry Inspection measurements for staircase depth or height, initially recorded in inches and feet, measurements were updated with four decimals! This explains why on top of the exit staircase of the Catacombs, Rue Rémy Dumoncel, one can read *"Profondeur 54 pieds / 17,5356 mètres"* ("Depth 54 feet / 17.5356 metres").

THE ATELIER

⬆ Rare "turned pillar"(or abandoned pillar) visible in the Catacombs, at the opening of the Ossuary's vestibule.

As a result of the many and often majestic works carried out by the Quarry Inspection Unit, there are only a few places left where one can observe the former quarrying zones, offering insight into limestone quarry techniques. The access path to the Ossuary of the Catacombs nevertheless affords one such interesting opportunity, in what has been dubbed "the Atelier", although it is located in a gallery rather than a genuine quarry void.

How did quarry workers go about digging galleries? The first technique, "room-and-pillar", simply consisted in boring quarry galler-ies running more or less parallel and intersected by perpendicular galleries: this had the effect of leaving large undisturbed masses of limestone, dubbed "turned pillars" (*piliers tournés* in the original French) because one can indeed turn around them. These pillars supported the quarry roof so as to prevent the hills from *"bowing down"*[24]. The main draw-back of the "room-and-pillar" method was that the limestone composing the pillars had to be surrendered in that it could not

---

24 L.-S. Mercier, *op. cit.*, vol. 2, chapter 189 *"Plancher d'une partie de la capitale"*, p.110.

↑ The Atelier's *hagues et bourrages* landscape. From time to time, a slight rumbling of the RER B train passing overhead can be heard.

be extracted. Moreover, underground drilling invariably generates a large quantity of waste, resulting from both the quarrying itself and on-the-spot stone cutting. Waste was left inside the quarry; this is why in the circulation galleries, visitors tread over roughly two metres' worth of backfill. Between the end of the 15th century and the beginning of the 16th century, quarry workers invented a new excavation technique: "dry stone wall and waste" (*technique par hagues et bourrages*). Only some of the limestone beds were fully exploited and the large ensuing voids were filled in with excavation waste as well as soil brought from the surface. Backfill was kept in place by dry-stone walls called *hagues* (which has the same etymology as the word "hedge" in English). These walls were consolidated here and there by pillars made of roughly cut limestone blocks piled up on top of one another by sheer human force, hence their name *piliers à bras* ("hand-made pillars" or "stacked pillars"). These pillars were also erected in places where the quarry roof was fissured and revealed structural weakness, such as in the Port-Mahon quarry.

⬆ Décure's sculpture. The round towers
in the background possibly represented
Minorca's windmills in the 18th century.

DÉCURE AND PORT-MAHON

Before entering the Ossuary, the path makes a small detour through a lower level, where one can admire sculptures dating back to the very early works carried out by the Quarry Inspection Unit.

There, one reads: *"Cet[te] ouvrage fut commencé en 1777 par Décure dit Beauséjour vétérant de sa Majesté et fut fini en 1782"* ("This work was begun in 1777 by Décure, also known as Beauséjour, veteran of His Majesty's army, and was completed in 1782"). The last two lines were superimposed on two older lines of writing which had been carefully "erased", more definitively than the *"te"* of *"cette"*.

A former soldier, Décure worked as a quarryman for the Quarry Inspection Unit. He had fought in Louis XV's army that the Duke of Richelieu had raised in 1756, in order to recover Minorca (Balearic Islands) and had subsequently sojourned in the Anglo-Spanish bunkers of Port Mahon. Port Mahon, the island's main harbour, was deemed to be the vastest and the most beautiful of the whole of the Mediterranean; as it was

The Port-Mahon Quarry

The mediaeval quarry near the sculptures was named after Port Mahon, a fact recalled by the presence of sign plates such as "Chemin de Port-Mahon" ("Path to Port Mahon"). In fact, this was the name by which it was classified as Historic Heritage in 1994. The sculptures themselves are not included in these protective measures, nor is the Ossuary. This site is threatened by a real-estate project overhead.

sheltered from the winds, it was a trade route port to the Levant. After serving in the army, Décure worked for the Quarry Inspection Unit from its inception. His time spent on a paradisiacal island, albeit against his will, earned him the ironic nickname "Beauséjour" (literally, "beautiful sojourn") coined by his fellow quarrymen. We owe him the faithful rendering of the citadel of Mahon, with great attention paid to details, leading him to use black flint stone tiles from the Meudon chalk quarry to depict the sea. He worked on this task from 1777 to 1782: while building a staircase to access his masterpiece, he was fatally injured by the collapse of the quarry roof. Despite the fact that this deadly accident had occurred while he was performing non-commissioned work, the Quarry Inspection Unit granted his widow an allowance for life.

⬆ First part of Décure's sculptures:
the Cazerne district, the former Hôpital
des Anglais where Décure was billeted.

During Guillaumot's era, the
Catacombs were already a
fashionable place to go, visited
by anyone who was someone on
their visits to Paris, even before
the Catacombs opened to the
public. During their subterranean
promenades, a few prominent
personalities paused for refresh-
ments at a table built by Décure:
the Count of Artois, one day to
become Charles X, accompanied
by some ladies of the Court, in
1787, followed by the Duchess of
Polignac and Madame de Guiche
in 1788.

⬆ Fort Saint-Philippe overlooking the
entrance of Port-Mahon.

↑ Access to the Quarrymen's Foot Bath, a well that today's guides can no longer use to play pranks on tourists.

THE QUARRYMEN'S FOOT BATH

After the sculptures by Décure, one walks past the "Quarrymen's Foot Bath". This water well is special because it permitted surveying of the Paris substrata; in a manner of speaking, it was the first geological drill to be carried out under Paris.

This well was dubbed the "Quarrymen's Foot Bath" because the water is so crystal-clear that the only way to detect its presence is to step into it. One can guess what fun a mischievous guide might have had with this feature, especially since before electricity was installed in 1974, candles and torches only lit the upper portion of the gallery so that the first step of the staircase—which is flooded by water—was concealed by the darkness.

THE OSSUARY

The opening of the Ossuary's vestibule.
Masonry on either side of the door, engraved
30 T 1876, was built under Inspector Tournaire.

MEMORIÆ MAJORUM

Visitors preparing to enter the Ossuary
(*Le Monde illustré*, 1865).

Itinerary highlights

1 Entrance vestibule
2 Plate commemorating the establishment of the Ossuary
3 Last bone transfers (1859)
4 Croix de Bordeaux
5 Samaritan Fountain
6 Memento Pillar
7 Sacellum Crypt (Altar)
8 Former entrance
9 Sepulchral Lamp
10 Imitation Pillar
11 Mineralogical Collection
12 Gilbert's Tomb
13 Osteopathological Cabinet
14 Le Mierre's Gallery
15 Monument to the September 1792 massacres
16 Lower Catacombs
17 Monument to the 1871 Paris Commune
18 Monuments commemorating the 1789 French Revolution
19 Monument dedicated to Prince Oscar of Sweden's visit
20 Bones from Madeleine Cemetery
21 Dame Legros's tombstone
22 Crypt of the Passion of Christ
23 Pillar of the Clementine Nights
24 Exit door (Door of the Tombe-Issoire)

Ossuary Tour Itinerary

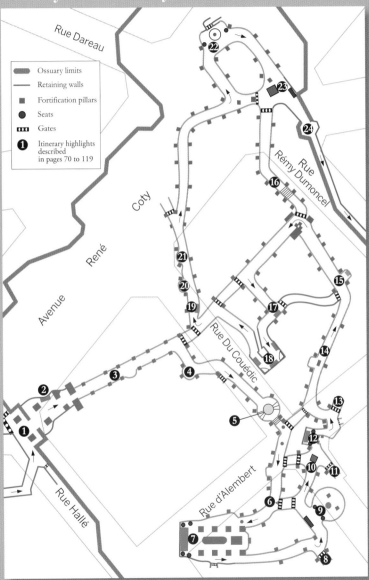

Rue Dareau

Rue Rémy Dumoncel

Coty

René

Avenue

Rue Du Couédic

Rue d'Alembert

Rue Hallé

Ossuary limits
Retaining walls
Fortification pillars
Seats
Gates
Itinerary highlights described in pages 70 to 119

↑ The famous verse by Jacques Delille which used to welcome visitors in the Ossuary vestibule: "Halt! This here is the empire of death".

The present-day vestibule

The entrance vestibule **1** to the Ossuary is located 14.34 metres below ground surface. The Parisian necropolis is delineated to the north by Rue Hallé, to the east by Avenue René Coty (formerly known as Avenue de Montsouris), to the south by Rue Dareau, and to the west, roughly by Rue d'Alembert. Visitors pause as they they read an engraved alexandrine rhyme: *"Arrête! C'est ici l'empire de la mort"* [25] (Halt! This here is the empire of death), by poet Jacques (the Abbot) Delille[26], buried in Père-Lachaise Cemetery. The first inscription one encounters (on the left) is a plate commemorating the establishment of the Ossuary **2**. This is not where the plate was originally affixed, since this entrance only dates back to 1859–1860. The plate was formerly located near the old entrance, where it was embedded in bones rather than affixed to a sustaining wall.

---

25 Very loosely translated from Virgil's original verse: *"Comprime gressum. Umbrarum hic locus est, somni noctisque soporae."*, in *The Aeneid*, book 6, verses 389-390.
26 Jacques Delille, *Œuvres de Jacques Delille: L'Énéide [de Virgile]*, Paris, L. G. Michaud, 1821, book 6 ("The Visit to the Underworld"), verses 126-129 ("Aeneas Requests Entry to Hades").

⬆ The motto on the lintel of the Ossuary's entrance door, *"Memoriae majorum"* (in memory of the ancestors), became that of Héricart de Thury.

⬇ Stele commemorating the creation of the Catacombs. It was moved from the original entrance to today's vestibule following the Ossuary's extension, renovations not mentioned by the engraved inscription.

Inside the quarries, three access doors for the Ossuary had been created in Héricart de Thury's days, each connected to a staircase: the first one was situated at the Barrière d'Enfer (the "Toll Gate of Hell" facing the present-day entrance on Place Denfert-Rochereau), the second on Rue de la Tombe-Issoire, the third on the Montsouris Plain (which corresponds to the Rémy-Dumoncel exit).

Today a visit of the Ossuary thus begins with the most recent bone transfers—those which

CATACOMBES ETABLIES PAR ORDRE DE M^r
THIROUX DE CROSNE L^{nt} G^{al} DE POLICE
PAR LES SOINS DE Mr Cte AXEL GUILLAUMOT
INSP^r G^{al} DES CARRIÈRES EN MDCCLXXXVI.
RESTAURÉES ET AUGMENTÉES PAR ORDRE
DE M^r LE Cte FROCHOT C^{er} D'ETAT.
PREFET DU DÉPARTEMENT DE LA SEINE
PAR Mr HERICART DE THURY ING^r EN CHEF
DES MINES INSP^r G^{al} DES CARRIÈRES.
MDCCCX.

↑ Bones from Saint-Nicolas-des-Champs Church, temporarily deposited in Vaugirard Cemetery.

justified the latest extension of the delivery area. On that occasion, Doctor Paul Broca conducted craniometric studies on bones inside the Catacombs, poring over skulls from the Saints-Innocents Cemetery, others from the Western Cemetery, as well as those from a cemetery on La Cité, predating the 13th century. These studies were the subject of a lecture given at the Society of Anthropology in July 1861.

First glimpses: the last bone transfers

❸ When crossing the threshold of the Ossuary itself, a relatively low-placed lintel forces the visitor to bend over as though in deference and humility, bearing the engraved inscription *"Memoriæ majorum"*[27] ("in memory of the ancestors" in Latin). The reverse side of the lintel reads: *"Quocumque ingrederis.*

---

27 *"Marcellum memoria majorum et preces Caesaris poenae magis quam infamiae exemere"* in Tacitus, *Annals*, vol. 14, chapter 40.

Sequitur mors, corporis umbra"[28] ("However thou enterest, Death shadowlike will follow thy every step").

Immediately upon entering the Ossuary, the visitor walks between two walls of bones—long bones such as tibias and femurs of which only the apophyses are vis- ible. These walls are ornamented with cranium-studded friezes arranged at different heights, protruding from the even surfaces of the walls to which they add a macabre yet romantic touch— some craniums are even arranged to portray the contours of a heart! The recess immediately after

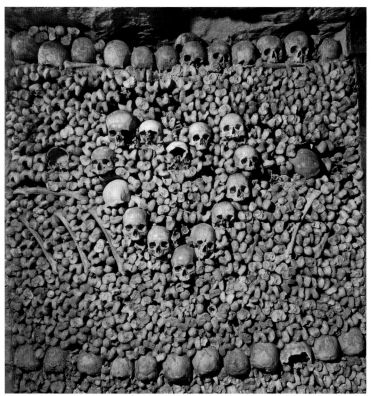

---

28 A misquote of Cato, *Distichs*, vol. 4, verse 37: *"Quocumque incedis, sequitur mors corporis umbra".*

⬆ A romantic yet macabre decorative detail: a heart of skulls.

⬆ The Croix de Bordeaux, whose copper plate was stolen in 1902.

the curve of the gallery towards the right is adorned with a stone cross, the Croix de Bordeaux ❹, a rare religious sign in the Ossuary. Less rare, however, than one might think, since other examples made from craniums can be observed. However, today it is barely possible to discern these forms from the rest of the bones. On this stone cross, a copper plate was once affixed, reading: "*Jacques de Bordeaux, Sr. De Saint-Aubin-sur-Yonne, Cons^er du Roy au Parlement, épousa demoiselle Madeleine Sauvat. Mort en 1593. David + Jésus.*" ("Jacques de Bordeaux, Lord of Saint-Aubin-sur-Yonne, Advisor to the King in Parliament, married the maiden Madeleine Sauvat. Deceased in 1593. David + Jesus"). The plate was stolen in 1902 [29].

---

29 É. Gérards, *op. cit.*, p.466.

↑ Detail from an old postcard.

The Samaritan Fountain

Following the present-day visitors' path, the next monument encountered is the Samaritan Fountain **5**. The term "fountain" is used broadly here to designate an architectural creation by Héricart de Thury dating from approximately 1810: the feature resembles a small basin to collect water falling to the ground. The Samaritan Fountain was also dubbed the "Spring of Lethe" or

SICUT UNDA
DIES NOSTRI FLUXERUNᵀ

the "Spring of Forgetfulness" by analogy with the mythological river of Hades, but these names have fallen into disuse. Its current name refers to the Biblical episode of the woman of Samaria to whom Jesus said: *"Whosoever drinketh of this water shall thirst again: But whosoever drinketh of the water that I shall give him shall never thirst; but the water that I shall give him shall be in him a well of water springing up into everlasting life."*[30] The visitor is reminded of this episode by an inscription of these Biblical verses in French (*"Quiconque boit de cette eau aura encore soif. Mais celui qui boira*

⬆ "Like waves, our days have washed away". Today's visitors turn their backs on this inscription when accessing the Samaritan Fountain; in the past, they would face it.

de l'eau que je lui donnerai n'aura point soif dans l'éternité; car l'eau que je lui donnerai deviendra en lui une fontaine intarissable pour la vie éternelle") on the pillar behind the Fountain. The citation in Latin was formerly also found on another pillar.

On 25 November 1813, four goldfish (also known as cyprinid fish or *Carassius auratus*) were introduced to the fountain. They failed to reproduce and were said to have gone blind. At the beginning of 1885, two cyprinid fish and one tench replaced them

---

30 *King James's Bible*, John 4:13-14.

QUICONQUE BOIT DE CETTE
EAU, AURA, ENCORE SOIF
AD LIEU QUE CELUI QUI
BOIRA DE L'EAU QUE JE
LUI DONNERAI, N'AURA
JAMAIS, SOIF
E+ JUANNA   IV

ANIMÆ QUIBUS ALTERA
FATO.
CORPORA DEBENTUR LETHÆI
AD FLUMINIS UNDAM.
SECUROS LATICES ET LONGA
OBLIVIA POTANT.
ÆNEID. LIB. VI.

The Samaritan Fountain, twice converted
into an "aquarium".

in the fountain, surviving until December 1886. The adding of the fish can be said to foreshadow the experiments taking place from 1897 onwards in "the Laboratory of the Catacombs of the Jardin des Plantes", set up by Armand Viré. This lab hosted the first biospeleological experiments to be conducted, but was damaged by the 1910 Great Flood of Paris: shortly thereafter, it ceased its activities. In the Ariège region in France, the Laboratory Moulis currently pursues similar studies on development modifications induced by the constraints of a subterranean environment.

↑ The Memento Pillar today, against a gate; on the roof, one of the old arrows.

↓ The Memento Pillar was designed in triangular form as it was positioned at the intersection of three galleries (Cloquet's engraving n°4).

This gigantic wheel made of bones had to make way for modern pillars before the Altar.

HOMO SICUT FENUM DIES EJUS:
TANQUAM FLOS AGRI SIC
EFFLOREBIT QUONIAM SPIRITUS
PERTRANSIBIT IN ILLO, ET NON
SUBSISTET ET NON COGNOSCET
AMPLIUS LOCUM SUUM.

PRINCIPIUM
ET FINIS

ETERNITE

HIC IN SOMNO PACIS
REQUIESCUNT MAJORES

The Altar for Mass leans against
a consolidation work which became
necessary in 1810.

The Altar and the Masses

On the left of the path leading to the Altar for Mass is the triangular pillar of the Memento **6**; on each of its sides is written *"Memento Homo, quia pulvis es, et inpulverem reverteris"* [31], a Biblical verse traditionally recited during Ash Wednesday Mass.

The Sacellum Crypt **7** is composed of two elements: the Grand Altar of the Obelisk (or else the Altar of the Obelisks) and the Great Cross, which in the present day is concealed by relatively modern pillars. This site was damaged by rockfall in

---

31   *Latin Vulgate Bible*, Genesis 3:19: "You are dust and to dust you shall return".

⬆ Mass in the Ossuary, a sufficiently rare and picturesque event to be recorded by several photo and television reports (Mass said by Monseigneur Touzé, 15 November 1950).

QUI DORMIUNT IN TERRÆ
PULVERE EVIGILABUNT
ALII IN VITAM ÆTERNAM,
ET ALII IN OPPROBRIUM.

↑ The Great Cross just opposite the Altar, today masked by modern pillars. The engraved text comes from the Book of Daniel: *"Many of them who sleep in the dust of the ground will awake, these to everlasting life, but the others to disgrace and everlasting contempt."*

1810, and the mass of rock placed there for consolidation purposes was fashioned in the shape of an altar. The Altar, once completely surrounded by bones, is a reproduction of an antique tomb discovered on the left bank of the Rhone River in 1807, between the French towns of Vienne and Valence; this discovery was no less than a major archaeological event. Upon it, one reads: "Asleep in death, here lie our ancestors"; above it: "Man sees his days wither like the hay: he shines for a brief moment, like a field flower; wind blows upon him, and he is no more, he knows not the place where he will be laid to rest". The very first bones transferred to the Catacombs in 1786 lie beside the Altar.

↑ Panoramic view of the Sepulchral Lamp Crypt; on the left, bones from Saint-Laurent Cemetery (see page 8).

Every year, on All Souls' Day (the day after All Saints' Day or All Hallows' Day), a mass was celebrated in this spot, up until the mid-1970s.

In this area, a magnificent wheel made from bones once stood, but was removed during recent refurbishments, also responsible for partially masking the Great Cross.

The Sepulchral Lamp

Just before reaching this section, a gate on the right-hand side sets apart the vestiges of the former entrance ❽ created in the days of Héricart de Thury. Although the corridor leading to the old vestibule is obstructed (it was adorned by two Tuscan pilasters on either side of a black door on which the words "*Has ultra metas resquiescunt beatam*

spem expectantes"[32] were inscribed), opposite, the black cross is still visible, weeping black tears of mourning.

As bones began to be stocked in large quantities in the Catacombs, the air often became rarefied. As a remedy, a fire was kept going in a bowl, which came to be known as the Sepulchral Lamp **9**, thus ensuring the renewal and circulation of air. In addition, bottomless bottles were embedded in the masonry of certain wells leading above ground; corks accessible from the quarries sealed the bottlenecks. According to the flow of air desired, workers uncorked the necessary number of bottles. In 1860, Paul Fassy mentions that "cross sections of calcare-

32 *"Beyond these bollards, they lie in wait of eternal bliss"* (copy of the inscription at the entrance of one of the two cemeteries of Saint-Sulpice Parish).

Has ultra metas
requiescunt beatam
spem expectantes

The Western Vestibule (former entrance to
the Ossuary) with, in the background, the
black cross with a quotation from Seneca
(Cloquet's engraving n° 1).

ous tufa rise in the middle of the crossroads".[33] What were these meant for? Perhaps, as was the case with the Sepulchral Lamp, to purge from the air of the stench due to the latest bone transfers. Later on, numerous service shafts built by the Quarry Inspection Unit rendered these rudimentary but efficient systems obsolete. In the 1980s, the surroundings of the Ossuary were walled in so as to sever all communication between the general gallery network and the actual Catacombs, and to prevent clandestine intrusions. This move upset

↑ The Sepulchral Lamp Crypt, by Cloquet (engraving n° 6).

← The black cross with tears of mourning and an engraved text, which once welcomed visitors, still stands.

atmospheric conditions and in 1995, air-conditioning had to be installed to prevent the degradation of the bones.

Upon leaving the site of the Sepulchral Lamp, one walks between bones from the Saint-Laurent Cemetery. In Héricart de Thury's days, these formed a crypt whose vault was supported by doric pilasters; inside it, a pedestal made from tibias was topped by a skull (cf. pp.8-9).

33 *"Des coupes taillées dans le tuf* [sic]*, s'élèvent au milieu des carrefours"* in Paul Fassy, *op. cit.*, p.33.

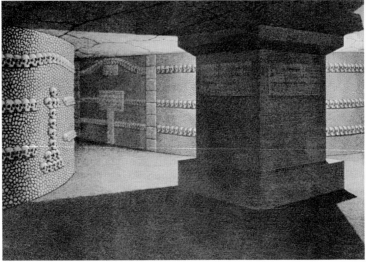

⬆ The Imitation Pillar today, and seen by
Cloquet (engraving n° 5).

The Lachrymatory Sarcophagus

⬆ Gilbert's Tomb, drawn by Cloquet (engraving n° 3).

Just before zigzagging past Gilbert's Tomb, visitors walk around the Imitation Pillar ❿, a sustaining pillar thus named because it is inscribed with four quotes from Thomas A'Kempis's book[34]. On each side of this square support pillar, one of the following maxims is engraved:

"Happy is the man who hath the hour of his death always before his eyes, and daily prepareth himself to die.

If thou hast ever seen one die, consider that thou also shalt pass away by the same road.

When it is morning reflect that it may be thou shalt not see the evening, and at eventide dare not to boast thyself of the morrow.

Ah, foolish one! Why thinkest thou that thou shalt live long, when thou art not sure of a single day?"[35]

---

34 Thomas A'Kempis, *Imitation de Jésus-Christ (français), traduite du latin... appropriée à toutes les communions chrétiennes.* Nouvelle édition, Paris, Grassart, 1884, vol. 1, chapter 23 *"De la méditation de la mort"*, verses 15-17 and 35.

35 Thomas A'Kempis, *Imitation of Jesus Christ,* Translated by Rev. William Benham, 1886.

In the past, to the right of this pillar, behind the gate, a geological cabinet of curiosities initially created by Héricart de Thury, the Mineralogical Collection of the Ossuary **11**, was visible. Inside the room, a fake staircase rose up to the quarry roof, displaying the geological cross-section of the

↑ A rare photograph showing the Ossuary's Mineralogy Collection Cabinet.

precise location upon which it was set. Five further similar examples existed in the Parisian quarries. On each step, rock samples from the Tombe-Issoire were placed, and the thickness of the geological stratum in question was specified. Around the room, fossils, concre-

tions (stalactites and stalagmites), as well as other curiosities uncovered during works in the Ossuary area, were exhibited. Today, nothing remains of this cabinet, and the space it once occupied has been completely filled in.

Gilbert's Tomb **12** (also formerly

Gilbert's Tomb with, to its left, bones from Saint-Nicolas-des-Champs and, to its right, bones from Blancs-Manteaux; it is a cross that is found on the monument, and not an amphora as in Cloquet's engraving (see page 91).

known as the Lachrymatory Sarcophagus) is a mere cenotaph bearing this name because words by the poet Nicolas-Joseph-Laurent Gilbert are engraved upon it. Once again, we are in the presence of a simple consolidation structure, shaped according to a

AU BANQUET DE LA VIE, INFORTUNÉ CONVIVE,

J'APPARUS UN JOUR, ET JE MEURS :

JE MEURS, ET SUR MA TOMBE, OÙ LENTEMENT J'ARRIVE,

NUL NE VIENDRA VERSER DES PLEURS.

⬆ The lines found at Gilbert's Tomb are also engraved at the Hôtel-Dieu where the poet wrote "*Stance sur la mort*" ("Stance on Death") one week before his death in 1780, at age 29.

suggestion from mining engineer Caly, who worked under Héricart de Thury. This empty tomb lying in the middle of bones without graves evokes freemasonry, just as the maxims and quotes scattered throughout the Ossuary remind us of the vacuity of life on earth. As a matter of fact, Charles-Axel Guillaumot, the first Quarry Inspector, was a member of "The Nine Sisters Lodge"[36], as was Benjamin Franklin, with whom he was acquainted. Nicolas-Joseph-Laurent Gilbert died in Paris on 2 November 1780, at the age of twenty-nine.

The words engraved on "his" cenotaph are a stanza from the Ode he wrote eight days before his death, inspired by several Psalms:

> "*At the banquet of life,*
> *unfortunate guest,*
> *I appeared one day, and now I die;*
> *I die, and upon my grave to where*
> *I slowly journey,*
> *None shall come to shed a tear.*"[37]

---

36 The Nine Sisters Masonic Lodge helped to organise French support for the American Revolution.

37 "*Au banquet de la vie, infortuné convive, // J'apparus un jour, et je meurs ; // Je meurs, et sur ma tombe où lentement j'arrive, // Nul ne viendra verser des pleurs.*" in Nicolas-Joseph-Laurent Gilbert, "*Ode IX imitée de plusieurs Psaumes*", Œuvres complètes de Gilbert / publiées pour la première fois avec les corrections de l'auteur et les variantes, accompagnées de notes littéraires et historiques, Paris, Dalibon, 1823, pp.132-133.

Le Mierre's Gallery

After leaving this mausoleum, visitors once arrived at the second cabinet of curiosities, this one devoted to osteopathology ⑬. Following the idea of Michel-Augustin Thouret[38], Héricart de Thury gathered in this part of the Ossuary all the strange anatomi-

↑ Start of Le Mierre's Gallery, sometimes also known as the Grand Gallery of the Catacombs; the verse comes from his poem "*Le jour des morts*" ("The Day of the Dead").

cal objects discovered while the bones were being arranged: a "pathological collection" of craniums and bones presenting fractures, cuts, necroses, calluses, fused bones, as well as oddly shaped specimens remarkable for their dimensions, shapes, or protuberances. In 1908, this cabinet was almost completely destroyed

---

38 During the excavation of graves from Saints-Innocents Cemetery, he studied the preservation of bodies in the form of dried or oiled mummies. He also took a keen interest in various bodily alterations caused by diseases and established a collection of rare anatomical specimens.

Quest-ce que chaque race!une ombre apres une ombre
Nous vivons un moment sur des siécles sans nombre
Nos tristes souvenirs vont s'éteindre avec nous
Une autre vie Ô temps, se dérobe à tes coups

Le mierre

↑ Another verse from the same poem by Le Mierre, "Le jour des morts", ends the gallery bearing his name.

after a collapse of the quarry roof. Moving on, we come across the gallery of dramatic poet Le Mierre **14**. Two quotes from his works frame the corridor. For instance, at the entrance, one reads: *"So many dead bodies stacked up and pressed against the earth! Numbers are meaningless here, the crowd is solitary".*[39] Further on, a poem by Rousseau (Jean-Baptiste, not Jean-Jacques), is offered for the visitor to ponder over: *"Our spirit is but a breeze, a passing shadow..."*[40] Many of the poets whose quotes are found throughout the Ossuary enjoyed a bout of fame in their time, but have since sunk into oblivion.

---

39 *"Que de morts entassés et pressés sur la terre ! Le nombre ici n'est rien, la foule est solitaire"* from "Le jour des morts" in Antoine-Marin Le Mierre, *Les Fastes, ou Les usages de l'année, poème en seize chants*, Paris, Gueffier, 1779, Chant XIV, pp.263-265.

40 *"Notre esprit n'est qu'un souffle, une ombre passagère..."* in Jean-Baptiste Rousseau, *"Épode tirée principalement des Livres de Salomon, et en partie de quelques autres endroits de l'Écriture et des prières de l'Église"*, *Œuvres lyriques de J. B. Rousseau*, Paris, J. Delalain, 1860, p.187. Here, the word *épode* means "final ode".

↑ Monument commemorating prison massacres in September 1792, much simpler than the initial project. Above it, an engraved plate.

The September 1792 massacres

Héricart de Thury wanted to pay a tribute to the men who fell during the French Revolution by building monumental memorial stones in the shape of antique tombs **15**. Not all the remains of the roughly one thousand prisoners massacred in Parisian prisons on 2 and 3 September 1792 were gathered inside the Catacombs. Some were laid to rest in cemeteries (Clamart Cemetery, Vaugirard Cemetery), others were thrown down a water well (Convent of the Carmelites), or left in the mass graves of the Bicêtre or the Salpêtrière Hospices, or even in an underground quarry, as was the case in Charenton. Due to some urban works and the closing down of cemeteries, some of these remains finally made it to the Catacombs.

Further along, the gate on the right-hand side used to open onto the staircase of the Lower Catacombs **16**. Opposite, at the turn of the path, the stone pillar once bore the date 1894, as well as the inscription: *"Cœur du*

← Top of the staircase to the Lower Catacombs, no longer open to the public, with an inscription in Latin: *"This here is the empire of death".*

↑ Staircase decorated with skulls, from the time when visits were supervised (*cf.* the Memento Pillar, Cloquet's engraving, p.78).

Général de Division / Baron Campi / mort à Lyon, le 14 octobre 1832 / Embaumé / par M. Jourdan, phar-macien" ("Heart of the General of the Division / Baron Campi / died in Lyon, on 14 October 1832 / Embalmed / by Monsieur Jourdan, chemist").

The heart of this General was found on 28 June 1893 during excavations on Avenue Niel. Locked in a heart-shaped leaden box and placed inside a small oak crate, it was deposited in the Catacombs on 9 May 1894, inside a niche dug inside this very pillar. It has since disappeared.

1870 and the battle inside the Catacombs

The siege of Paris by the Prussians began on 19 September 1870 and ended with the capitulation of Paris on 28 January 1871; the victory of the German Empire was proclaimed in Versailles. Civil war ensued, as the people of Paris took up arms against the government that had just signed the peace treaty, and seized the Hôtel de Ville. Parisians, rebelling against the people of Versailles, self-proclaimed themselves "Communards". An article from the magazine *L'Illustration* dated Saturday 17 June 1871 evokes an underground episode from the end of the insurrection (see next pages).

It is more than likely that this manhunt did not actually take place in the Ossuary, but rather in the disused underground quarries often improperly designated by the same term "Catacombs". In fact, people in Paris used the word "Catacombs" long before their actual creation. As early as 1782 (the Ossuary was established on 7 April 1786), an anonymous publication sold in novelty stores was entitled *Projet de catacombes pour la Ville de Paris, en adaptant à cet usage les carrières qui se trouvent tant dans son enceinte que dans*

→ This is the only monument in the Ossuary to mention an event relating to the 1871 Paris Commune. The single word *"Déposés"* (deposited) replaced the ancient inscription *"Violés par les fédérés"* (violated by the Communards).

ses environs (literally: *Catacombs Project for the City of Paris, by Adapting to this Purpose the Quarries Situated Within the City Limits as well as in its Vicinity*). While certain events actually did occur in the old underground quarries in 1870–1871, it is likely that they mostly took place either in the "Carrières d'Amérique" or in the vast network stretching from the Luxembourg Gardens to the southern suburbs of Montrouge, Bagneux, and Issy-les-Moulineaux. The journalist from *L'Illustration* most certainly extrapolated a fight in the Ossuary from reading other articles mentioning a manhunt for the Communards in the Parisian underground.

17 Only one monument in the Ossuary refers to the 1871 Paris Commune; this monument, indicating bones from Saint-Laurent Church, was apparently first conceived for an expiatory chapel above ground. Two corrections have been made to the engrav-

ings: the word *"ossemens"* (bones) which replaces another word, while between two letters ("V" and "S"), a stone plate has been embedded which bears the inscription *"déposés"* ("laid to rest"). Émile Gérards, in *Paris souterrain*, mentions the fact that around 1880, a polemical inscription *"violés par les fédérés"* ("violated by the Communards") was masked. The letters "v" and "s" are all that is left of the original inscription.[41] The adjective "violated" referred to the "tombs", the word replaced by "bones".

---

41 É. Gérards, *op. cit.*, pp.457-458.

Manhunt in the Catacombs

"This manhunt in the Catacombs constitutes one of the most dramatic episodes of the tragedy that was the storming of Paris by the Versailles army. We should therefore preserve its memory by a drawing and a few words.

Battles in the city streets are over. The insurgents have been ousted from all their positions. All those who were not killed in combat, imprisoned, or executed, have sought to save themselves by taking flight. Some took shelter in the sewers, others in the "Carrières d'Amérique"*, others finally, in greater numbers, in the Catacombs.

None of these refuges protected them for long. Hunted down and struck on all sides, they were all killed on the spot or imprisoned and transported to Versailles. The manhunt in the Catacombs began in the first days of this month. Troops entered through the door of the Toll Gate of Hell, while other troops stood guard in front of the other door opening onto Montsouris Plain. Then, torch-bearing soldiers carefully descended into the immense Ossuary. What took place next is an easy guess.

Our illustration is all too eloquent for us to feel the need to add superfluous words to describe it. How ghastly this supreme struggle must have been, in the crimson torchlight strangely lighting the tense faces of the combatants! Furious stamping feet, cries of anger and cries of pain, death rattles, the clicking of the bayonets, detonations; what a scene! All this took place in the long corridors of these bone-lined crypts, under the watchful eyes of the dead, troubled in the sleep that had been promised them! Indeed, the words "*Beyond these bollards, they lie in wait of eternal bliss*" are written in Latin above the door one passes through to enter their underground home: "*Has ultra metas requiescunt beatam spem expectantes.*"

L'Illustration, 17 June 1871.

* The "American Quarries" were gypsum quarries located in the present-day 19th arrondissement. One hypothesis for the adjective "American" was that it referred to the owner of these quarries, an Irishman by the name of Fitz-Merald who had sought wealth in America and had purchased these quarries upon his return to France.

Monuments commemorating 1789

⓲ Following the reference to the Paris Commune, a monumental triptych takes a step back in time by recalling three events associated with the French Revolution. On 28 and 29 August 1788, violent combats broke out on Place de Grève (Place de l'Hôtel de Ville) after the resignation of the Minister of Finance Loménie de Brienne: victims were buried a few days later in the Ossuary, which hosted for the very first time whole bodies and not just bones.

On 28 April 1789, the Réveillon wallpaper manufacture, in Faubourg Saint-Antoine, was ransacked and torched. The owner had allegedly declared that a worker could survive on fifteen pennies a day, thus provoking his employees to rebel. The bodies of the workmen who perished during the riot were exposed for five days in the Catacombs so that their kin might identify them; they were then covered in quicklime and buried.

⬇ French Revolution Crypt: on the right, the monument recalling 1788, on the bottom left corner, that of 1789, and facing left, that of 1792.

↑ Sign commemorating the official visit of Prince Oscar of Sweden in 1867, undoubtedly during the Universal Exposition.

On 10 August 1792, nearly 2,000 people—Swiss Guards, as well as common folk and noblemen—were killed in a battle that took place at the Tuileries. Not all those who fell were granted the honour of the Catacombs: some of them were buried in an abandoned gypsum quarry at the bottom of Montmartre hill (around the present-day Rue d'Orsel). In 1992, an expiatory mass was organized in memory of the Swiss Guards who perished at the Tuileries; it was the first in a series of events organized for the official bicentennial commemoration of the death of Louis XVI.

The monument dedicated to Prince Oscar of Sweden's visit

19 Moving towards the sector of the bone transfers dating back to 1859, the first monument one encounters on the right commemorates a private visit by Prince Oscar of Sweden[42] in the presence of the Archpriest of Upsaal, on 7 May 1867, during the Universal Exposition. Prior to this event, visits to the Catacombs had occurred on a quarterly basis; during it they took place weekly. The influx of visitors from all over the world (52 million visitors attended the great Universal Exposition of 1900) had reper-

---

42 The future King Oscar II of Sweden.

cussions on the Parisian underground. In 1889, there were 20,003 visitors and 18,463 in 1900, whereas the average number in years when no Exposition was being held did not exceed 10,000 visitors. From the 1930s until the 1950s, the number of visitors fell to 6,000–7,000 visitors for an average of 100 opening days per year. Today, however, the Catacombs receive 250,000 visitors every year.

Bones from the Madeleine Cemetery

20 Next come bones from the Madeleine Cemetery (Rue de la Ville l'Évêque). Similarly to other bones arriving at the Ossuary in 1859, they first transited through the Ossuary of the West in 1844, also known as the Vaugirard Cemetery, situated at n°6 Rue Vaugirard. This 1859 bone deposit was made famous by a self-portrait by Félix Tournachon, also known as Nadar. Taking advantage of the latest adjustments to the Ossuary, Nadar tried his hand at photographing in artificial light conditions thanks to the invention of electric light, in the Catacombs as well as in the Paris Sewers. He thus produced the first underground photographic reportage.

⬇ Numerous guillotine victims including Louis XVI and Marie-Antoinette were buried at Madeleine Cemetery where an "Expiatory Chapel" was then built.

OSSEMENTS DE L'ANCIEN
CIMETIÈRE DE LA MAGDELEINE
(RUE DE LA VILLE LÉVÊQUE Nᵒˢ 1 et 2)
DÉPOSÉS EN 1844 DANS L'OSSUAIRE
DE L'OUEST ET TRANSFÉRÉS DANS LES
CATACOMBES EN SEPTEMBRE 1859.

OSSEMENTS DE L'ANCIEN
CIMETIÈRE DE LA MAGDELEINE
(RUE DE LA VILLE L'ÉVÊQUE N° 1–
DÉPOSÉS EN 1844 DANS L'OSSUAIR
DE L'OUEST ET TRANSFÉRÉS DANS L
CATACOMBES EN SEPTEMBRE 185

Ecce homo: 1861 self-portrait by Félix
Tournachon, better known as Nadar, a
forerunner in underground photography.
The slightly blurry face is due to the long
exposure time necessary for the shot

In the space of three months, Nadar took about one hundred shots of the Catacombs and the Sewers. He also wished to photograph the workers in action, not only out of a taste for the picturesque, but also to give a sense of the scale and proportions of the galleries, lacking from prior depictions of the Catacombs. As a shot required up to 18 minutes of perfect stillness (those were the days of the wet collodion photographic process), Nadar settled for the use of life-size dummies, which he generally posed with their backs to the camera, due to their lack of realistic features: *"It would have been difficult for me to obtain absolute inorganic stillness from a human being. I tried to overcome the difficulty with mannequins that I dressed as workmen and positioned as best I could in the setting…"*[43] Nevertheless, the photographer himself endured the exercise of prolonged immobility for a single self-portrait on which his face appears only very slightly blurred. This historical photo session took place in front of the bones from the old Madeleine Cemetery.

Dame Legros's tombstone

㉑ Upon the closure of several Parisian cemeteries, several funerary monuments were stored in the courtyard of the Tombe-Issoire House (from which bones were lifted down into the quarry), but Dame Legros's tombstone was the only one ever to be incorporated into the Ossuary. The following words were inscribed on it: *"À la mémoire de Françoise Gellain, Dame Legros, couronnée par l'Académie française en 1784, morte le 12 décembre 1821; 73 ans"* ("In memory of Françoise Gellain, Dame Legros, awarded a prize by the Académie Française in 1784, deceased on 12 December 1821; 73 years old"). During her lifetime, this lady became infatuated with a prisoner, Jean-Henri Masers de Latude (1725–1805), who had spent around thirty-five years in various gaols. Escaping several times, he was caught again each time. Françoise Gellain finally succeeded in having him freed. Latude remained the most famous prisoner of the Bastille throughout the 18th century[44].

---

43 Philippe Néagu & Jean-Jacques Poulet-Allamagny, *Le Paris souterrain de Félix Nadar. 1861: Des os et des eaux* (catalogue of the exhibition organised by Paris-Audiovisuel, in the context of the "Mois de la Photo"), Paris, Caisse Nationale des Monuments Historiques et des Sites, 1982, p.59.

44 As the story would have it, Dame Legros had fallen in love with the intrepid Latude without ever having encountered him: she had simply caught a note he had cast down from a window. She made it her life's purpose to free him, and for this, was awarded a Prize for Virtue in 1784.

À LA MÉMOIRE

DE

DAME FRANÇOISE GELLAIN,

DAME LEGROS,

COURONNÉE PAR L'ACADÉMIE FRANÇAISE,

EN 1784,

DÉCÉDÉE À PARIS LE 12 X.BRE 1821,
AGÉE DE 73 ANS.
SON EPOUX,

SES ENFANS, SA FAMILLE, SES AMIS.

ICI REPOSE EN PAIX CETTE FEMME ADMIRABLE
QUI DE LATUDE ENFIN FIT OUVRIR LES CACHOTS,
TRENTE DEUX ANS DE FER, O FEMME INCOMPARABLE
EXCITENT TA PITIÉ POUR TOI PLUS DE REPOS.
APRÈS TROIS ANS ET PLUS, PAR TA PERSÉVÉRANCE
TU SUS L'EN ARRACHER, L'EUROPE T'ADMIRA,
LE PRIX DE LA VERTU COURONNA TA CONSTANCE
ET LA POSTÉRITÉ JAMAIS NE T'OUBLIERA.

Engraved tombstone, the only one to make its way down to the Ossuary (in 1860). Marked Françoise Gellain, the only person to be mentioned by name amongst the remains.

Detail from the start of the descent between
Dame Legros's tombstone and the Barrel.

➡ The Barrel in the Crypt of the Passion, the venue of a famous clandestine concert in April 1897.

The Crypt of the Passion of Christ

The gallery of the Ossuary then slopes down considerably, enabling the visitor to reach the bottom of the gallery of the Lower Catacombs (which is fitted with a staircase to overcome this difference in height).

Next, the visitor enters the Crypt of the Passion of Christ ㉒ in which a quotation from *The Gospel According to John* is engraved behind the gate leading to the emergency stairs: *"Consummatum est / Tout est consommé"* ("It is finished" [45]). However, the most significant monument there is the Barrel, a steel pillar around which bones have been arranged to resemble a giant vat. Beyond the gate, the path leads to the well into which bones were thrown down from the courtyard of the Tombe-Issoire House. To prevent bones from getting stuck during their

---

45 *King James's Bible*, John 19:30. The last words pronounced by Christ on the Cross before expiring.

← Start of the slope downwards to the Lower Catacombs, and beyond, the exit vestibule.

↗ Shaft for lowering bones: overhead was the Tombe-Issoire House where a few remarkable funerary monuments were stored until 1794.

descent when cartloads were emptied into the well, whenever necessary, workers could shake a large chain hanging inside the well to loosen them.

It was in this very Crypt that a clandestine concert was organised between midnight and 2 a.m. on 2 April 1897. This event, drawing about a hundred patrons, was only made possible by the collusion of two workers of the Quarry Inspection Unit. When their involvement was discovered, they were obviously dismissed... but reinstated shortly thereafter. The repertoire of the concert befitted the circumstances: Chopin's *Funeral March*, and that of Beethoven's *Heroic Symphony*, the chorale and funeral march from composer Xavier Ledoux's *Les Perses*[46], and Camille Saint-Saëns's *Danse macabre* (based on a poem written by Henri Cazalis). Poems were recited: Alla's "Ave Maria", Marlit's "Aux catacombes", as well as some verses by Henri Cazalis.

---

46 Xavier Ledoux, *Les Perses: tragédie antique, suite d'Orchestre*, Paris, Leduc.

The 1897 concert, a "musical and profane" event in the words of the invitation card (*Le Monde illustré*, 10 April 1897).

← The Pillar of the Clementine Nights that prevented the roof from falling in further and turning into a subsidence sinkhole.

The Pillar of the Clementine Nights

❷❸ Just before exiting the Ossuary, visitors can observe a massive square pillar, with a text engraved on each of its sides, as in the case of the aforementioned Imitation Pillar, except that this one is much wider. This is the Pillar of the Clementine Nights, thus named because it is inscribed with the Italian poem dedicated to the death of Pope Clement XIV, "*Notti Clementine*", by Giorgi Bertola.[47]

While visiting the Catacombs on 16 May 1814, Francis I, the Emperor of Austria, took particular notice of the monument commemorating the massacres of September 1792. When he reached the Pillar of the Clementine Nights, he repeated several times the two concluding sentences of one of the stanzas from "*Notti Clementine*":

"Speak up, ye horrid remnants!
What is left now of the honour
and rank ye boast'd!
Is not the inequality among men
pure folly?
What is become of these great
names and their glowing
pageantry?
When released from the transient
muck of this mortal coil,
How shall we tell the herdsman
from the mighty monarch?"

↑ *"At death we leave everything behind"*, from the Book of Ecclesiastes or Ben Sira's *Book of Wisdom*.

---

47 "*Parlate, orridi avansi ! or che rimane // Dei vantati d'onor gradi, e contrasti! // Non son follie disuguaglianze umane ? // Ove son tanti nomi, e tanti fasti ? // E poichè andar del mortal fango scarchi // Che distingue i pastor dai gran monarchi.*" in Aurelio de' Giorgi Bertola, *Le notti Clementine*, Arezzo, Michele Bellotti, 1775, Canto 1, st. 6. Clement XIV was born Giovanni Vincenzo Antonio Ganganelli.

Last philosophical reminder before passing through the "Tombe-Issoire" exit (or Lower Catacombs vestibule): *"Stimulus autem mortis peccatum est"* (*"The sting of death is sin"*, from the First Letter to the Corinthians 15:56).

The exit door

㉔ To the left, before the Ossuary's exit door, a plate bears the old spelling of "Tombe-Issoire" (with a "Y", as in Tombe-Yssoire,), which was later corrected, as was also the case with some of the inscriptions marking bones from Saint-Innocents (spelt "Ynnocents"). On this spot itself, the visitor stands 16.02 metres below ground level. On the lintel, a verse by Cato is engraved: *"Whomever despiseth life, feareth not death"[48]*. After passing through this door (known as the Door of the Tombe-Issoire), one comes across a translation of a passage from Ezekiel[49] by French poet and Marquis of Pompignan, Jean-Jacques Le Franc, inscribed on the right wall of the gallery:

---

48 *"Non metuit mortem, qui scit contemnere vitam"* in Cato, Distichs, book 4, verse 22.
49 *"Ossa arida, audite verbum Domini..."*, in *Latin Vulgate Bible*, Ezekiel 37:4-6.

"Ecoutez Ossemens arides,
Ecoutez la voi du Seigneur.
Le Dieu puissant de nos ancêtres
Qui d'un souffle créa les êtres
Rejoindra vos nœuds séparés.
Vous reprendrez des chairs nouvelles
La peau se formera sur elles
Ossemens secs, vous revivrez"[50].
The corresponding Latin verses
could once be seen opposite this
wall. Unfortunately, in this sector
it is possible to view damage and
vandalism wreaked by disrespect-
ful visitors wishing to leave traces
of their passage by writing on the
walls.

In the days of Héricart de Thury,
the visit ended with another
inscription, translated from Virgil
by Jacques Delille, an authority
on the Roman poet:

"Il n'est que trop aisé de descendre
aux enfers;
Les palais de Pluton nuit et jours
sont ouverts:
Mais rentrer dans la vie et revoir la
lumière,
Est un bonheur bien rare, un vœu
bien téméraire."[51]

⬆ The inscription *"Memoriae majorum"* is also found on the back of the lintel of the Ossuary's exit door, which once served as an entrance door.

⬇ French version of the "Ossa Arida" monument inspired by Ezechiel, in the vestibule of the Ossuary exit.

("The path to hell is easy:
black Dis's door is open night and
day:
but to retrace your steps, and go
out to the air above,
that is work, that is the task." [52])

---

50 *"O ye dry bones, hear the word of the LORD. Thus saith the Lord GOD unto these bones; Behold, I will cause breath to enter into you, and ye shall live: And I will lay sinews upon you, and will bring up flesh upon you, and cover you with skin, and put breath in you, and ye shall live; and ye shall know that I am the LORD"*, Saint James's Bible.
51 Delille, *op. cit.*, book 6 ("The Visit to the Underworld"), verses 126-129 ("Aeneas Requests Entry to Hades").

52 Translated by A. S. Kline, 2002.

The bell atop this column echoes the term *cloche de fontis*, an example of which is found overhead.

A long corridor, posterior to 1870 (therefore more than ten years after Paris's annexation of the town of Montrouge), leads directly to the foot of a staircase built in the 18th century, opening onto the Voie Creuse (later renamed Rue des Catacombes, then Rue Dareau in 1858, and finally Rue Rémy Dumoncel in the present day).

THE FONTIS GALLERY

In this gallery (entirely consolidated between 1874 and 1875), the visitor walks past various subsidence sinkholes, three of which are over ten metres deep. Two are presented in a highly pedagogical and astute manner: after removing from the ground all the rubble from land collapsing in the quarry, the walls of these subsidence pits, instead of being masked by masonry retaining walls, were simply consolidated using sprayed cement. Moreover, coloured lines marking the different geological strata cut through by the sinkhole were painted directly on the sprayed cement. On top of the last coloured line, the date 1875 was stencilled... as if in a mirror! At the base of the gallery, an obelisk column built in

⬆ In the exit gallery, the Fontis Gallery: indications of a backfilled gallery, and a subsidence sinkhole.

1937 (therefore at the same time as the conversion of this gallery into a civil defence shelter) is topped by a "bell", reminding the visitor of the French expression used to describe the collapse of a quarry roof: *cloche de fontis*, due to the bell shape it naturally acquires once stabilized.

The last subsidence pit also bears a stencilled date, 1874, but it is partially masked by an openwork arch in millstone grit, serving as a foundation system for a building constructed right above it.

ORIGINAL EXIT STAIRCASE

To reach the surface (and to exit at n°36, Rue Rémy Dumoncel), visitors must climb a spiral staircase, whose narrowness never fails to surprise. Unlike the entrance staircase, the exit staircase dates back to the origins of the Catacombs; it was built under the supervision of Quarry Inspector Charles-Axel Guillaumot in 1784, as one may guess by seeing the inscription at the top indicating its depth: 54 feet. Exiting visitors turn their backs upon this inscription, only intended as information for workmen using the staircase while on duty. It is the same inscription as that previously alluded to, whose conversion from the inch-feet to the metric system comically resulted in a four-decimal figure (17.5356 metres). When reaching the top of this staircase, one cannot but admire the superb monolithic slabs covering the ceiling. The aedicule —at which visitors arrive and from which they immediately exit to step into the street—is embedded into a structure that was added during works to align building facades on the street. One can only imagine what life must have been like with this easement in the middle of the Montrouge Plain countryside. Indeed, the Ossuary of the Catacombs is one of the rare sections of the public quarries under Paris (if not the only one) which was not located under the public domain, but under private properties. When the quarries were converted into the Catacombs, galleries located under the former village of Montrouge were filled with bones. Above ground, the area has in fact preserved its village-like aspect to this day, observable when taking a stroll along Rue Hallé, Villa Hallé and other adjacent streets.

The journey we have just undertaken stretches across 1,500 metres, of which only 600 metres proceed between walls of bones of the Ossuary as such. Below ground, the notion of distance is considerably altered by the nature of the surroundings—closed horizons, extremely narrow galleries compared with the width of surface streets—so that the same distance always appears longer below ground than above ground, all the more so as the path meanders considerably.

➔ Top of the exit staircase. Visitors turn their backs on this inscription indicating depth as they climb the stairs.

Acknowledgments

Erwann Benoit, from the Comptoir des Catacombes, without whom this project would never have taken off;

Catherine Decaure, from the Musée Carnavalet, who allowed us access to the Ossuary to take the photographs for this work;

Emmanuel Gaffard, artificial underground photographer, and his assistant Clotilde Richalet;

Claude Huguet, from the PICAR association, a great collector of old documents on the quarries and the Catacombs of Paris;

Diane Langlumé, for her lively participation in the project, as well as Fui Lee Luk, for her attentive proofreading;

Tristan Pimpaneau, bookshop owner and booklover with a passion for Parisian quarries, with whom I discussed questions requiring specialised knowledge;

Christopher Spence, English tour guide specialising in the history of Paris and amateur palaeontologist;

Roland Michel Tremblay, whose photos of the Catacombs accompanied me throughout the writing of this guide...

... and of course the team at Parigramme, François Besse, whose trust I am grateful for, Laurence Solnais, Isabelle Chemin and Julie Hiet, with whom it was a pleasure to prepare this book.

The Catacombs of Paris

www.catacombes.paris.fr
1, avenue du Colonel–Henri-Rol-Tanguy, 75014 Paris
Tel.: 01 43 22 47 63 - Fax: 01 43 22 48 17
Open daily from 10 a.m. to 5 p.m. (last admission at 4 p.m.),
except Mondays and bank holidays.

Don't forget to check if the Museum is open before your visit just in case it is closed for technical reasons.
Watch out ! There is no access for people with limited mobility (131 steps to go down, 83 steps to go back up, 112 for the emergency exit).

See also: *www.catacombes-de-paris.fr*

Further reading on the Paris underground

ARCHER Caroline, *Paris Underground*, New York, Mark Batty, 2005.

BROADWELL Valerie, *City of Light / City of Dark (Exploring Paris Below)*, Bloomington, XLibris, 2007.

GAFFARD Emmanuel, *Paris souterrain: carrières, catacombes, cryptes, égouts, tunnels / Beneath Paris: Quarries, Catacombs, Crypts, Sewers, Tunnels* (bilingual edition), Paris, Parigramme, 2007.

HOVEY Tamara, *Paris Underground*, New York, Orchard Books, 1991.

MARSHALL Alex, *Beneath the Metropolis*, New York, Carroll & Graf, 2006.

PIKE David L., *Subterranean Cities. The World Beneath Paris and London (1800–1945)*, Ithaca, Cornell University Press, 2005.

SHEA Neil & ALVEREZ Stephen (photographer), "Under Paris: Secrets Beneath the Streets", *National Geographic*, vol. 219, n°2, February 2011, pp.104-125.

THOMAS Gilles & CLÉMENT Alain (editors), *Atlas du Paris souterrain* (winner of the Haussmann Prize 2002), Paris, Parigramme, 2001.

Also worth a look:

www.anarchistecouronne.com: a web site presenting a broad range of photos of the Catacombs through the eyes of Quebecois writer Roland Michel Tremblay, author of *Denfert-Rochereau* (iDLivre Éditeur, 2001).

www.lutecia.fr: the web site of the PICAR association (Institute for the Safeguarding and Rehabilitation of Industrial Quarry Heritage)

Copyrights

Editorial coordination: Laurence Solnais
With the collaboration of Fui Lee Luk

Art direction & layout: Isabelle Chemin

Maps: Julie Hiet

Printed in UE in October 2014

ISBN: 978-2-84096-721-7

(Dépôt légal: juillet 2011)